A New Library of
the Supernatural

Alchemy, the Ancient Science

Alchemy, the Ancient Science

by Neil Powell

**Doubleday and Company, Inc.
Garden City, New York, 1976**

EDITORIAL CONSULTANTS:

COLIN WILSON
DR. CHRISTOPHER EVANS

Series Coordinator: John Mason
Design Director: Günter Radtke
Picture Editor: Peter Cook
Editor: Sally Burningham
Copy Editor: Mitzi Bales
Research: Sarah Waters
General Consultant: Beppie Harrison

Library of Congress Cataloging in Publication Data

Powell, Neil
Alchemy, the Ancient Science
(A New Library of the Supernatural)
1. Alchemy   I. Title   II. Series
CD13.P68   540'.1   76-23791
ISBN 0-385-11323-4

Doubleday and Company
ISBN: 0-385-11323-4
Library of Congress Catalog
Card No. 76-23791
A New Library of the Supernatural
ISBN: 11327-7

© 1976 Aldus Books Limited, London
D. L. S.S.: 317/76
Printed and bound in Spain
by TONSA San Sebastián
and RONER Madrid

**Frontispiece: 17th-century alchemist by Van Ostade.
Above: porcelain caricature figurines of alchemists.**

Alchemy, the Ancient Science

For centuries a number of men of science and learning spent their lives in the practice of alchemy, searching for a way to change ordinary metals into gold. Why did they try? Did any of them succeed? We know that alchemists today continue the old tradition and the age-old quest. Will they succeed?

Contents

1

The Meaning of Alchemy

It is late at night. In a room hidden away from prying eyes, an old man bends over a flask of bubbling colored liquid. All around is a clutter of jars, bottles, and apparatus that looks somewhat like the equipment in a modern school chemistry laboratory. The walls are hung with animal skulls and astrologers' charts. A stuffed owl sits amid a jumble of thick leatherbound books with iron clasps. From time to time he stirs the liquid, muttering strange words to himself. His fur-collared cloak is in tatters, and he shivers slightly from the chill draft leaking through a broken window. His supper, entirely forgotten and long cold, lies untouched

Absorbed in the long labor of a dual search—for the secret that will enable him to transmute base metal into gold and to achieve spiritual perfection—the alchemist pursued his involved experiments, laying the foundations for the science, then still unborn, that we now know as chemistry. Often his experiments had unexpected results: sometimes a new element would be isolated, sometimes a mixture went up with a bang.

Right: *Explosion in the Alchemist's Laboratory*, a painting that shows the dangerous result of a sudden and violent chemical reaction.

"The whole of his adult life has been devoted to a single task"

on a nearby bench. Nothing disturbs his concentration as he patiently watches the liquid evaporate. Then disappointment clouds his face. Something has gone wrong. He pores over an old manuscript, puzzling at the strange language and symbols. With a sigh, he sets up some more apparatus. Perhaps a grain more of this and a grain less of that? His excitement returns. The years have slipped by unnoticed. His whole life has been dedicated to one task. He is determined to discover the secret of turning ordinary metals into gold.

Although there is some truth in this popular description of an alchemist, it is by no means the whole story. There is far more to alchemy than a desire to make gold, and serious alchemists were not crazy old men. They were often among the leading scientific and religious thinkers of their time.

The word *alchemy* is an Arabic one, but no one is wholly sure where it came from. The most popular explanation is that it originally meant "the art of the land of Khem." *Khem* was the name the Arabs gave to Egypt, and it was from Egypt that they acquired their knowledge of this strange science, which they later transmitted to the West. Another possibility is that the word derives from the Greek *chymia*, which means the art of melting and alloying metals.

Alchemy is extremely complicated. It is based on the practical skills of early metalworkers and craftsmen, on Greek philosophy, and on Eastern mystic cults that sprang up in the first centuries after Christ and influenced so much of magic and occult thought. It must be remembered that when alchemy flourished there was no dividing line between science and magic. Ideas such as the influence of the planets and the effect of certain numbers or letters on people's lives might today be regarded as superstitions. At that time they were perfectly acceptable to those who were making the kind of accurate observations about the material world that paved the way for modern science.

Long before the beginning of alchemy gold was regarded as the most valuable metal. Its possession indicated wealth and power, and it was prized for its beauty. Known as the most perfect metal, it soon acquired symbolic meaning. It came to stand for excellence, wisdom, light, and perfection. For serious alchemists gold had both a real and a symbolic significance, which at first seems confusing. The reason is that alchemists embarked on two different and difficult quests at the same time, and success in one meant success in the other. The first aim is the one that most people know about. The alchemist was attempting to find a way of transmuting, or changing, ordinary metals into the most perfect metal, gold. The second aim is less well-known but was far more important. The alchemist was trying to make the soul progress from its ordinary state to one of spiritual perfection.

For many centuries Western alchemists ceaselessly searched for the Philosopher's Stone. What was this elusive object? It was not some giant boulder on which ancient sages sat and meditated. Nor was it a closely guarded tablet inscribed with words of wisdom. It was a substance that alchemists were convinced they could make, with divine assistance, by subjecting certain raw materials to complex and lengthy chemical pro-

Above: the obvious goal of alchemy and the best-remembered one was the production of gold from base metal. Here in a 19th-century engraving, executed long after alchemy had lost its preeminent position as a respectable science, an alchemist displays a small nugget of gold to his patron.

Left: the Spanish mystic Raimon Lull, traditionally believed to have been an alchemist. Whereas the making of gold has been well remembered by posterity, the second, hidden part of the quest is mainly forgotten. The alchemist was also searching for a way to reach spiritual perfection, and believed that purifying base metals into the "perfect" metal, gold, was the outward symbol of transmutation of his soul from an ordinary state to a condition of union with God. In this illustration, Lull holds a newborn baby—the personification of the soul.

9

Left: *The Alchemists* by Pietro Longhi, painted about 1757. The alchemist on the right points to the Philosopher's Stone, the gold-colored magical liquid that could be produced only by a series of mysterious, intricate processes. Below: a detail from the painting showing the retort that was called the Philosopher's Egg, in which it was believed the Universal Spirit could be given a material form as the strange gold-making essence sought after by so many.

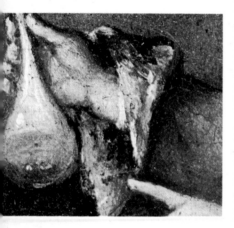

cesses. The problem was to find the right raw materials and the correct chemical processes. It was a widely held belief that the Universe was permeated by a spirit that linked everything together. Alchemists thought that this spirit could somehow be reproduced and compressed into a magical substance which they named the Philosopher's Stone. Once discovered, a small quantity of this magical substance added to ordinary metal would change it into gold. Taken as a medicine, the Stone would act as a miraculous cure. It was even believed by some to confer immortality, and was often called the Elixir of Life.

All the patient experiments that alchemists carried out in their laboratories over the centuries were motivated by one overwhelming desire—to produce the Philosopher's Stone. In the course of their painstaking and dedicated work they established many important chemical facts which, even if they did not lead to the Philosopher's Stone, helped to form the basis of chemistry as we know it today.

The greatest alchemists were skilled in many fields. The scope of knowledge in those days was small enough that a person might hope to master all there was to know about subjects as diverse as medicine and religion, philosophy and alchemy, logic and magic. The seeker of knowledge would see nothing incompatible in the different fields of study. Magic would not conflict with medicine, or philosophy with religion. Knowledge was thought of as a unity, and all the different branches were different aspects of this unity. They all led toward a greater understanding of the Universe.

Above: *The Elixir of Life* by the 19th-century caricaturist Phiz. Medieval alchemists believed that the transmuting agent—the Philosopher's Stone—would also act as a universal cure if taken as a medicine, ending disease and old age by conferring immortality upon the fortunate beings who drank the magical and elusive substance.

Roger Bacon, the Scholar Alchemist

Roger Bacon was a medieval scholar of wide learning. Although some of his supposed inventions have been shown to be purely legendary—he did not, for example, invent gunpowder—he was certainly well ahead of his time in many ways. Two of his suggestions that show his many-sided brilliance were that imperfect sight could be aided by using suitably shaped lenses, and that the globe could be circumnavigated. It was perhaps this gift of thinking beyond others of his time which led to the idea that Bacon was aided by the Devil, and because of his willingness to oppose many of the notions current at the time, he suffered persecution.

In his alchemical work Bacon distinguished between theoretical alchemy and practical alchemy. He believed practical alchemy superior to other sciences, and more likely to produce material advantages. Like the other medieval thinkers, he thought experiments did not provide a basis for inferring general laws, but only gave confirmation of conclusions that are reached by deduction from already accepted general principles.

In this respect, Bacon was a man of his time. That reasoning lies behind much of the traditional alchemical work.

The greatest Arab alchemist, Jabir, who lived from about A.D. 722 to 815, was a widely read scholar who wrote treatises on an enormous variety of subjects including geometry, poetry, magic squares, and logic. Although his main concern as an alchemist was discovering how to convert ordinary metals to gold, he also recorded many important chemical observations, and his design of apparatus led to the development of the modern still.

Al-Razi, the celebrated Persian alchemist and physician who lived from about A.D. 866 to 925, wrote books on medicine, natural science, mathematics, astronomy, logic, philosophy, and theology, as well as many works on alchemy. For the first time in the history of chemistry, facts about chemical substances, reactions, and apparatus are carefully observed and verified in his books.

When we come to 13th-century Europe we find Albertus Magnus among a distinguished selection of alchemists. He was one of the greatest scholars and teachers of the Middle Ages, and as recently as 1932 was canonized as a Catholic saint. Among his many works were treatises on alchemy, and he was the first to describe the chemical composition of such substances as cinnabar, white lead, and minium.

Below: even Cleopatra was considered by tradition to have been an alchemist, as shown in this illustration of her gold-making process, from a Coptic manuscript of the 3rd century A.D. Part of the inscription reads, "One is All, and through it is All, and by it is All" and "if you have not All, All is nothing."

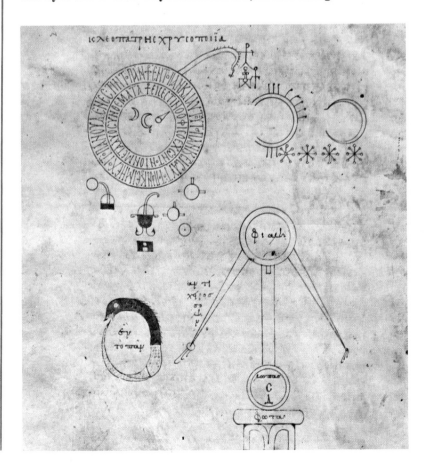

Far right: Albertus Magnus, 13th-
century scholar and churchman.
His alchemical writings show his
interest in a field of study that
during his lifetime was considered
fully worthy of investigation by
the best and most pious thinkers.
Below: Saint Thomas Aquinas,
who died in 1274, was a pupil of
Albertus Magnus, and like his
master believed in the possibility
of making gold alchemically. But
he held that the occult operations
of a celestial virtue were needed.

NOS ARABES FLAMMAS, SCOPULOS, NEPTUNIA PUBES
Colliculos Celsos NOMINAT ARMA DARES.

Above: a symbolic synthesis of the Great Work, from a 17th-century French alchemical manuscript. The central figure is probably Nature, or Flora, uniting the powers of darkness and light (indicated by the dresses). The alchemist is sitting to the left under the tree with his scale beside him. The faces in the hollow tree behind him are probably past alchemists, whose accumulated wisdom helps him in his quest. The difficulty that the reader encounters in trying to unravel the symbolism of alchemy is largely intentional: it was meant to be obscure, to be deciphered only by those who had "eyes to see" and were capable of understanding the mystic message.

Paracelsus was one of the most notable scientific figures of the 15th century. From his knowledge of alchemy he was able to introduce a whole new range of medicines for medical treatment. Until that time remedies had been almost exclusively herbal.

One of the greatest difficulties encountered in exploring the development of alchemy is that the books and manuscripts describing the substances to be used and the chemical processes to be followed were written in such obscure, symbolic language. They were often open to many different interpretations, and were puzzling even to an experienced alchemist. An ordinary reader would be floundering after the first sentence. Because the books that the alchemists consulted are incomprehensible to all but an initiated few, most of our knowledge of alchemy is based on legends of transmutations. Many of these have been handed down and greatly embroidered in the course of time. At this distance it is impossible to gauge how much truth there might have been in these stories, and how much trickery. However, there are some accounts that appear convincing. These are ones

in which the narrator has an established professional reputation and little to gain from deceiving others. One such man was the well-known Dutch physician Johann Friedrich Schweitzer, who lived in the 17th century.

Schweitzer, who was born in 1625, was a distinguished doctor. He numbered Prince William of Orange, the future King of England, among his patients. In the fashion of his day, he was generally known by the Latin version of his name, Helvetius. In 1666 when he was 41 years of age, Helvetius received a strange Christmas present: the ability to turn lead into gold. He later wrote down an account of what happened. On December 27, in the late afternoon, a stranger came to his house. He described him as being "of a mean stature, a little long face, with a few

Above: the need—as alchemists saw it—to conceal their arts from all but each other led to a weird literature in which fantastic creatures were used as symbols only intelligible to the initiated. In this manuscript of 1572 a dragon resuscitated after death stands for one specific process.

Left: the alchemist Leonhard Thurneysser being visited in his laboratory by his patron, the Elector Johann Georg. Fraud was hardly an unknown in alchemical circles, and Thurneysser had an interesting line of trickery. He would take an iron nail and offer to transmute half of it to gold. He dipped the nail into an oily liquid, and presto! as he withdrew it, half of it was golden. The secret was simply to start with a nail that was already half iron and half gold, paint it black, and then dip it into a solvent. The paint dissolved, and the rapt audience saw the "transmutation."

15

Below: Johann Schweitzer, known as Helvetius. He was a well-respected doctor of medicine, the physician to the Prince of Orange. His account of a transmutation is still one of the most circumstantial and puzzling alchemical reports, with apparently little opportunity and no motive for fraud.

small pock holes, and most black hair, not at all curled, a beardless chin, about three or four and forty years of age (as I guessed) and born in North Holland." The stranger told Helvetius that he had read several of his pamphlets, and in particular one that was highly critical of an English experimenter who had claimed to have invented a universal medicine. Did Helvetius think, asked the stranger, that it was impossible?

The two argued in a friendly fashion for some time. Then the stranger took out of his inner pocket a carved ivory box and showed Helvetius its contents—three heavy pieces of stone "each about the bigness of a small walnut, transparent, of a pale brimstone color." This, said he, was enough to turn some 20 tons of lead into gold. Helvetius handled a piece greedily, and begged the stranger to give him just a little. When the stranger told him that this was impossible, he contrived to scrape a speck under his fingernail surreptitiously.

After telling Helvetius how he himself had learned the art, the stranger demonstrated "some curious arts in the fire," and promised to return in three weeks' time. As soon as he was gone, Helvetius excitedly got out a crucible and melted some lead in it. When he added the tiny crumb of stone, however, "almost the whole mass of lead flew away," leaving only a dull residue.

The physician impatiently awaited the return of the stranger, more than half convinced that he would not come again; but in three weeks exactly the man of mystery once more came to his house. "But," said Helvetius, "he was very sparing in speaking of the great elixir, gravely asserting, that was only to magnify the sweet fame of the most glorious God." Again the physician begged him for some of the stone, and at last the stranger relented. According to Helvetius: "He gave me a crumb as big as a rape or turnip seed, saying, receive this small parcel of the greatest treasure in the world, which truly few kings or princes have ever known or seen." Ungratefully Helvetius protested that this was hardly enough to transmute four grains of lead, whereupon the stranger took it back, divided it in half, and flung half in the fire saying, "It is yet sufficient for thee."

Helvetius confessed his former theft, and recounted his lack of success. The stranger laughed and said: "Thou art more dextrous to commit theft, than to apply thy Tincture; for if thou hadst only wrapped up thy stolen prey in yellow wax, to preserve it from the arising fumes of lead, it would have penetrated to the bottom of the lead, and transmuted it to gold." He promised to come again the next morning at nine to show Helvetius the proper procedure.

"But the next day he came not, nor ever since; only he sent an excuse at half an hour past nine that morning, by reason of his great business, and promised to come at three in the afternoon, but never came, nor have I heard of him since; whereupon I began to doubt of the whole matter. Nevertheless late that night my wife . . . came soliciting and vexing me to make experiment of that little spark of his bounty in that art, whereby to be more assured of the truth; saying to me, unless this be done, I shall have no rest nor sleep all this night . . . She being so earnest, I commanded a fire to be made (thinking alas) now is this man (though so divine in discourse) found guilty of falsehood . . . My

Left: illustration from *Ordinall of Alchimy*, a 15th-century text by Thomas Norton. (Bodleian Library, Oxford, MS Ashmole 971, f.14v). It shows a pupil learning the mysteries of alchemy from a master, which was the usual way of becoming an alchemist oneself. The experience of Helvetius was startlingly different: he achieved success in alchemy without going through a long apprenticeship, having gained special powers and knowledge from a strange visitor.

wife wrapped the said matter in wax, and I cut half an ounce or six drams of old lead, and put it into a crucible in the fire, which being melted, my wife put in the said Medicine made up into a small pill or button, which presently made such a hissing and bubbling in its perfect operation, that within a quarter of an hour all the mass of lead was totally transmuted into the best and finest gold . . ."

The philosopher Spinoza, who lived nearby, came to examine the gold, and was convinced of the truth of Helvetius' story. The Assay Master of the province, a certain Mr. Porelius, tested the metal and pronounced it genuine.

What Helvetius implied in his story was that the strange visitor was an alchemist who had given him some of the Philosopher's Stone. Although we may find the idea incredible, and wonder whether Helvetius was the perpetrator of a giant hoax, none of his contemporaries saw it in that light. To them, alchemy was perfectly acceptable, and they saw no reason to doubt Helvetius' integrity.

What would an alchemist's laboratory have looked like at the time of Helvetius? We can gain a good idea from the many 16th- and 17th-century engravings and paintings of the subject. The

IOÁNES
STRATENSIS
FLANDRVS

walls of the room would probably be covered with strange symbols and alchemical inscriptions in Latin, Greek, Hebrew, or Arabic. Animal skeletons and bunches of medicinal herbs might hang from the ceiling. The tables would be piled high with books and parchments, jostling for space with retorts and crucibles and the odd human skull. There would be several different furnaces to provide different heats, and a bellows to fan the flames. There might be a glass mask for protecting the face, and there would be shelves filled with numerous jars, stills, and tripods. Of course, for the true alchemist, an altar for prayer and meditation was an essential feature. The room would probably be tucked away somewhere in the cellar or attic, where a gleam of light showing late at night would not attract too much attention. Alchemists were always anxious to preserve secrecy about their work. If too many people knew about their activities they might be persecuted by the Church for their strange beliefs, or hounded by greedy people hoping to amass a fortune.

Alchemists used a bewildering variety of ingredients in their search for the Philosopher's Stone. Copper and lead, sulfur and arsenic, urine and bile were but a few of them. Substances were combined and separated, heated and cooled, vaporized and solidified, and sometimes even just left to rot. The processes carried out in the laboratory were often fairly complex. Calcination, sublimation, and distillation are three of the better known ones. In *calcination* metals and minerals were reduced to a fine powder. In *sublimation* a substance was heated until it vaporized, and then returned to its solid state by rapidly cooling the vapor. In *distillation* a liquid was converted into a vapor by boiling, and then condensed back into a liquid by cooling. These and many of the other processes required heat, so furnaces were the most important equipment in the alchemist's laboratory.

Because the alchemist needed many different intensities of heat for his various operations, he had to have many furnaces of different sizes. Regulating heat was always a great problem. Thomas Norton, an English alchemist of the 15th century, is said to have invented dampers to regulate the heat of the furnace.

The fire of the furnace, which might be fueled with anything from charcoal and peat to rushes and animal dung, needed constant attention. Many alchemists believed that transmutation would be easier if very high temperatures could be obtained. They used the bellows to such an extent that they earned the nickname of "puffer." Now this term is used more appropriately to describe those who were searching only for gold, and not the true alchemist who also aimed at spiritual perfection.

Many chemical treatises give instructions on the use of different kinds of furnaces. Besides the calcinatory furnaces for reducing metals and minerals to a fine powder, there was the *athanor*. This contained a deep pan of sifted ashes. The material to be heated was placed in a firmly sealed container and covered with the ashes. This method is rather like a modern chemist's sand bath. Then there was the *descensory furnace*, which had a funnel with a lid. Liquid could flow down the stem of the funnel into a receptacle. Another sort of furnace was known as the *dissolving furnace*. It consisted of a small furnace supporting a pan full of water. In the pan were rings to hold glass containers. It

Above: an alchemist's oven or athanor, from a fresco executed about 1400. The alchemist's furnace was the most important piece of equipment, for exact degrees of heat were considered crucial for the stages of transmutation.

resembles a modern water bath, and is thought to have been invented by a woman alchemist who lived some time in the early centuries after Christ. She is a shadowy figure who appears in much of the mystical alchemical literature, and is known as Mary the Prophetess. She is also sometimes wrongly referred to as the sister of Moses. The French water bath or *bain-marie* is named after her.

Distillation was an important process in alchemy, and required a large number of different stills. The earliest stills were fairly simple. They consisted of a flask containing the substance to be distilled, a lid or still head, and a delivery spout leading to another flask that would receive the distilled liquid. The Arabs greatly improved methods of distillation. The word *alembic*, which we use today for part of a still, derives from the Arabic. The Arabs perfected the art of distilling the essence of flowers, fruit, and leaves. The invention of more complex stills in the 12th and 13th centuries, which included cooling mechanisms, led to the distillation of comparatively pure alcohol, and the discovery of many new substances.

Alchemists subscribed to one strange belief that made their

Left: the alchemist's water bath or *bain-marie*, a woodcut of 1519. The substances in the glass vessels suspended in the water were warmed only gradually by the furnace below the bath.

Left: Mary the Prophetess, also known as Mary the Jewess, an early female alchemist who was credited with the invention of the water bath that still carries her name. Traditionally she was believed to be Miriam, the sister of Moses. This stylized portrait was published in the 17th century.

Right: frontispiece of a treatise by Johann Rudolf Glauber, an alchemist who is now recognized as the greatest practitioner of practical chemistry of the 17th century. It shows a furnace with its parts, used for distillation.

A. the furnace itself, with an iron distilling vessel inside, fastened to a globular vessel that received the distillate.
B. the alchemist taking off the lid of the distilling vessel in order to spoon in some material.
C. the distilling vessel itself.
D. a cutaway view of the distilling vessel.
E. a second distilling vessel, not incorporated within a furnace.

tasks even more time consuming. Even when they thought that they had found the right substance and the right method of treating it for any stage in their experiment, they were convinced that they must submit the same substance to the same process over and over again. A special still, known as a *pelican*, was especially useful in this respect because it enabled a substance that had been distilled to be returned to its residue, and then to be redistilled as often as the alchemist desired. In some cases this was hundreds of times.

One of the oddest named pieces of equipment was the *Philosopher's Egg*. It was a *retort*—that is, a vessel into which substances are distilled—but an especially important one. The alchemist hoped that it would eventually contain the substance that constituted the Philosopher's Stone. It could then be said, in the strange allegorical language of alchemy that so often mixed the symbolic and the mundane, that the Stone had hatched from the Egg.

An alchemist's laboratory was a fascinating place, and alchemy exercised a hold over a wide range of people from learned religious and scientific thinkers to humble smiths and tinkers. Even reigning monarchs could be included among its practitioners. Charles II of England, who might be thought to have been fully occupied with foreign and domestic affairs, had a laboratory constructed under the royal bedchamber. Access was by a private staircase, Herakleios I, the 7th-century emperor of Byzantium, neglected his duties in later years to pursue his studies of alchemy. And Rudolf II, who was Holy Roman Emperor from 1576 to 1611, was financially ruined by his expenditures on astrology and alchemy.

Why was alchemy such a compelling subject? At first sight it seems to be an odd blend of the bizarre and the practical. The stories of transmutations are incredible, bordering on fairy tales, but the equipment that the alchemist used in his laboratory was technically advanced for its time. Why were such sophisticated scientific methods used in the pursuit of such mystical ideas? What were the beliefs that lay behind this occult science?

Right: *The Alchemist's Experiment Takes Fire,* by the 17th-century Dutch artist Hendrick Heerschop, shows a scene that was probably far from uncommon since alchemists worked with processes and materials whose explosive potential was only partially understood.

Below: the Neapolitan alchemist Giambattiste della Porta, writing in the late 16th century, came up with the interesting theory that the artificer of alchemical equipment should consider nature, "who hath given angry and furious creatures as the lion and bear thick bodies and short necks." Thus vessels to contain materials "of a flatulent nature and vaporous" should be large and low. Delicate spirits, however, should be drawn through long slender necks, like the ostrich—"gentle creatures and of thin spirits."

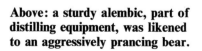

Above: a sturdy alembic, part of distilling equipment, was likened to an aggressively prancing bear.

Above: the pelican, with two necks for continuous distillation, took its name from the bird.

Above: the retort, another long-necked piece of equipment, was likened to a kind of wild goose.

2

The Principles of Alchemy

Prince Khalid ibn Yazid lived in Damascus in the 7th century A.D. Although he was the rightful caliph, he had been so sickened by political intrigue that he had retired from court and devoted his life to a study of alchemy. One day a manuscript that was supposed to contain the secrets of the Philosopher's Stone fell into his hands. Khalid studied it long and carefully, but was unable to understand it. He offered a magnificent reward to anyone who could solve the riddle of the manuscript and perform a successful transmutation.

Charlatans and rogues flocked to the Prince's house in Damascus. They ate his

The Arabs, who preserved so much of the classical Western tradition while Europe was mired in the economic and social disasters of the Dark Ages, included alchemy among sciences that they studied. Above: Jabir ibn Hayyan, most famous of the Arab alchemists. Right: page from an 18th-century Arab alchemical manuscript. The two large figures represent the sun and the moon, and the small figures between them probably represent metals. The inscription below explains that substances in balance are stable; only those not in balance will undergo change.

"Khalid... ordered the immediate execution of all the false alchemists"

food and spent his money and not one of them made the least progress in interpreting the manuscript. At that time Morienus, a true alchemist, was living a simple life as a hermit in Jerusalem. When he heard how the Prince was being deceived he was determined to visit him. He hoped not only to enlighten Khalid about alchemy, but also to convert him to Christianity. The Prince received him warmly and gave him a house and equipment for his work. In a fairly short time Morienus succeeded in producing the magic substance. He presented it to the Prince in a vase inscribed with the words "He who possesses this has no need of others." Khalid was overjoyed and ordered the immediate execution of all the false alchemists. In the ensuing commotion Morienus disappeared, and Khalid found that although he had the Philosopher's Stone, he had no idea how to use it. His servants searched far and wide, and eventually traced Morienus to his hermitage in Jerusalem. He returned to the palace of the Prince and initiated him into the secrets of alchemy. Khalid preserved what he had learned in a series of alchemical poems known as *The Book of Amulets, The Great and Small Books of the Scroll,* and *The Paradise of Wisdom.*

The story of Morienus is told in the first alchemy text that appeared in medieval Europe. This was the *Book of the Composition of Alchemy,* which was translated from Arabic into Latin in 1144 by an Englishman known as Robert of Chester.

It had been because of the Arab interest in learning that many Greek writings, including those on alchemy, were preserved. Within a century of the death of Muhammad, founder of Islam, the Arab empire reached from the Pyrenees to the Indus and incorporated hundreds of different tribes and races. Arabic had been made the official language, and all learned books were either translated into Arabic or written in Arabic. The city of Alexandria, an ancient Greek center of learning, had been conquered by the Arabs in A.D. 641. Its enormous library had already been partly destroyed. The Arabs eagerly seized what was left and later sent many of the books to Baghdad. In this way Arabic translations of Greek philosophers found their way all over the Arabic world, while for over 500 years the writings of the Greeks were almost unknown in Western Europe.

One of the most influential writers whose work was rediscovered in the library in Alexandria was Aristotle. His ideas had a particular influence on the development of alchemy. According to Aristotle, the basis of the entire material world was something that he called *prime* or *first matter.* This was not, as it may sound, some gray sludge from which the world gradually evolved. In fact, it was not a substance one could see or touch. It had no physical existence on its own account. However, it was the one unchangeable reality behind the ever-changing material world. To give this matter a physical identity and individual characteristics, various stages of *form* were needed.

The first stage of form, Aristotle believed, was found in the four elements of Earth, Air, Fire, and Water. The elements, while distinguished from each other, are also related by four qualities. These qualities are dry, moist, hot, and cold. Each element possesses two qualities, of which one predominates, and each element is linked to two other elements by the quality

Above: Morienus, who had been a Christian scholar in Alexandria before he became a hermit. He instructed the Arab prince, Khalid.

Above: soldiers of the Roman emperor Diocletian burning Egyptian alchemical books about A.D. 290. Apparently some alchemists who had mastered the art of preparing alloys that resembled gold and silver were passing off their good imitations as genuine metals. To end the nuisance, Diocletian ordered all the ancient books "which treated of the admirable art of making gold and silver" to be burned. As a result, we now have only a very few Egyptian technical manuscripts—those saved from the flames by chance. Two show clearly that the Egyptians were expert in metallurgy, which was a secret craft controlled by their powerful priesthood.

Left: a learned discussion in an Arab library. It was in libraries like this that the knowledge of the Greek philosophers was preserved during the long years when learning in Europe languished. This manuscript illustration dates from 1237, when Western learning lived only in a few monasteries.

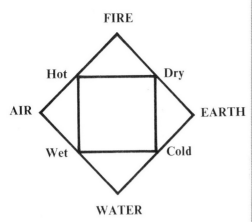

FIRE

Hot   Dry

AIR   EARTH

Wet   Cold

WATER

Above: the four elements and their qualities according to the theory of Aristotle, which formed the basis of the idea of transmutation—the changing of one element or material into another. The four elements were linked by the four qualities, each element possessing two qualities, both of which linked it to another element. This made it possible for it to change into either of them by the action of the quality that they shared between them.

Right: German medieval paintings of the four elements. These four elements also played a part in astrology, which was closely linked with alchemy at that time.

Fire

Air

Water

Earth

they possess in common. Here is how this system applies:

  Fire is hot and dry with heat predominating.

  Air is hot and moist with moistness predominating.

  Water is moist and cold with cold predominating.

  Earth is cold and dry with dryness predominating.

The diagram opposite shows the complex interrelationship of these qualities more clearly.

The main interest of Aristotle's theory of the elements from the point of view of alchemy is the idea of change. According to his theory each element can be transformed into another element through the quality they possess in common. In this way Fire can become Air through the action of heat; Air can become Water through the action of moistness; Water can become

Left: the four elements symbolized as an eagle (Earth), angel (Water), lion (Air), and bull (Fire), in a 17th-century German manuscript illustrating an alchemical poem. (Bodleian Library, Oxford, MS Add.A.287 f.23). In the multi-layered fashion which was typical of alchemical writing and thought, these four symbols were also used to stand for the four evangelists. This connected the Aristotelian concepts into the fabric of the medieval Christian theology, and provided yet another set of symbols for alchemists to use in their half-veiled explanations of the processes and materials they experimented with in their quest.

Earth through the action of coldness; and Earth can become Fire through the action of dryness. It is possible under this theory for an element gradually to complete the circle of change and go from Fire to Air, from Air to Water, from Water to Earth, and from Earth back to Fire, for example. It must be remembered that in all these changes the prime matter behind the form always remains the same.

The next stage of form in Aristotle's theory was that all physical manifestations in the world are composed of all four elements in different proportions. The varying amount of each element in the composition accounts for the infinite variety of things in the world. Because it was believed that elements could be transformed into other elements, it was only a small step to the assumption that all substances could be changed by altering the proportions of elements that constitute them. It is easy to see how alchemists took up this idea. If, as they believed, lead and gold both consisted of different proportions of the same four elements, what was there to prevent the one being transformed into the other?

Aristotle had another theory that influenced the ideas of alchemists. This was on the formation of metals and minerals. He believed that when the Sun's rays fell on water, they produced a vaporous exhalation that was moist and cold. This

Left: an alchemical process being carried out with the moon in Aries, from a woodcut illustrating a German text of 1519. Alchemists believed that the planets had the power of maturing metals in the earth, and so had an influence on alchemical operations that aimed at transmutation. Since the seven planets were believed to be associated with the seven metals, "favorable" times for experiments came to be when the right planet would be in exactly the right position.

exhalation became imprisoned in the dry earth, was compressed, and finally was converted to metal. All metals that are fusible or malleable, such as iron, copper, or gold, were, according to Aristotle, formed in this way. The formation of minerals, on the other hand, occurred when the Sun's rays fell on dry land. They produced a smoky exhalation that was hot and dry, and the action of the heat produced the minerals. In this category Aristotle included substances that cannot be melted, as well as substances such as sulfur.

The alchemists not only inherited Aristotle's attempts to explain the nature of the Universe, but were also greatly influenced by the elaborate astrological beliefs of the Ancient World. In fact, astrology and alchemy were so closely linked that many practicing alchemists were also astrologers.

From earliest times men have looked to the skies for explanations of their own lives, and the idea of the influence of the planets was widespread. Gradually, over centuries, in places such as Mesopotamia and Greece, a complex astrological system was built up. Its ideas permeated all aspects of daily life.

The basis of astrology can be summed up in the phrase so often quoted in occult literature, and in particular in alchemy: "as above, so below." This meant that everything in the Universe, or Macrocosm, had its parallel in the earthly world, or Microcosm. Everything worked in an ordered harmonious system, and everything was permeated by a Universal Spirit. It was this Spirit, which held the secret of the Universe, that the alchemists were trying to capture and compress into the Philosopher's Stone.

The system of correspondences, or connections, between the seven planets known to the Ancient World and all aspects of life was also extremely important. Tangible objects such as metals, animals, and plants, concepts such as colors, and abstract ideas such as love and wisdom were accorded to different planets, among which the ancients included the Sun and Moon.

Right: the mountain of the Adepts, an illustration of an alchemical book published in Germany in 1654. The complex symbolism of the picture relates the four elements shown by their Latin names, with the union of the King and Queen —under the signs of the sun and moon and the crowned eagle, which symbolizes Mercury—achieved in the heart of the mountain after the seven alchemical steps, or processes. Up the sides of the mountain stand the personifications of the seven planets (which also symbolize the seven metals) under the sun signs, which are given with their alchemical symbols. The two adepts at the bottom seem to symbolize the two paths of enlightenment in alchemy. One, blindfolded, is seeking divine inspiration, and the other, who is apparently observing two rabbits, has chosen the path of nature, presumably experimentation.

IGNIS.

AERIS.

AQVÆ.

TERRÆ.

V. WIWV.

TINCTVR.
COAGVLATION.
DISTILLATION.
PVTREFACTION.
SOLVTION.
SVBLIMATION.
CALTINATION.

RC. Sculp.

31

Above: Jabir ibn Hayyan in his chamber, being visited by a group including Muhammad (with his head in flames). Jabir was an important scholar and doctor as well as a practicing alchemist. It is reported that a large chunk of gold was found in his laboratory, rediscovered after his death. Could Jabir have made a successful transmutation?

Right: in a 14th-century work on alchemy an Arab is shown unlocking the gate to a town, probably symbolizing knowledge. The Arab contribution to alchemy was fully recognized by European alchemists.

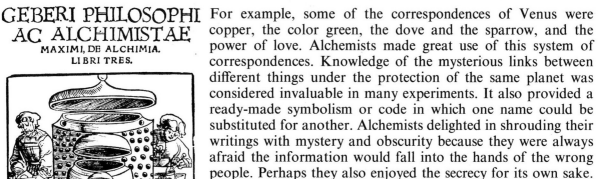

GEBERI PHILOSOPHI
AC ALCHIMISTAE
MAXIMI, DE ALCHIMIA.
LIBRI TRES.

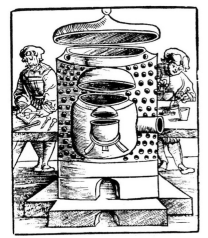

Above: the title page of a Latin
work on alchemy attributed to
Jabir, whose name is shown here
in the Western form of Geber. He
was recognized as the Father of
Alchemy, and his reputation was
so high that probably many books
by other authors were attributed
to him to give added authority.
How many of them were actually
written by Jabir is still vigor-
ously debated by many scholars.

For example, some of the correspondences of Venus were copper, the color green, the dove and the sparrow, and the power of love. Alchemists made great use of this system of correspondences. Knowledge of the mysterious links between different things under the protection of the same planet was considered invaluable in many experiments. It also provided a ready-made symbolism or code in which one name could be substituted for another. Alchemists delighted in shrouding their writings with mystery and obscurity because they were always afraid the information would fall into the hands of the wrong people. Perhaps they also enjoyed the secrecy for its own sake.

Since astrology was an integral part of everyday life in much of the Ancient World, craftsmen incorporated many of its beliefs into their work. Horoscopes were frequently used to determine favorable conditions for preparing certain drugs or metal alloys. Calculations often involved the use of strange mystic numbers and magic squares. When alchemists took over the chemical skills and metalworking techniques of the ancient craftsmen, they also adopted their astrological practices and belief in the power of numbers.

When the Arabs conquered Egypt in the 7th century A.D. they came into contact with many practicing alchemists, and were able to learn their skills and ideas at first hand. One of the earliest Arab philosophers to benefit from the contact was Jabir ibn Hayyan, who lived in the 8th century A.D. He made his own significant contribution to the theory of alchemy—one which survived in one form or another until well into the 18th century. He observed that metals and minerals appeared to be comprised of an "earthy smoke" and a "watery vapor." The first consisted of "atoms" of earth on the way to becoming fire, the second of water on the way to becoming air. He thought that these two components were not immediately turned into metals and minerals when imprisoned in the bowels of the earth; one was converted into sulfur, and the other into mercury, both of which were then thought to be kinds of elemental building blocks. Different proportions gave birth to different metals, and only if the sulfur and mercury were completely pure did they produce gold. Since other metals were the result of the inclusion of impurities, the removal of these impurities must finally result in the production of gold.

Many thousands of miles away on the other side of the world, the Chinese were also experimenting in alchemy. From this distance in time it is impossible to decide whether alchemy originated in the West and spread to China, or sprang up in China and spread to the West. It may be, of course, that it developed in both places independently. There were certainly some similarities between Western and Eastern alchemy. The Chinese also wanted to discover the secret of immortality, even though they were not on the whole as concerned with trans-muting base metals into gold.

One of the main differences was that, in place of the four elements defined by Aristotle, the Chinese designated five: water, fire, wood, metal, and earth. In addition, they recognized the principles of yang and yin instead of Jabir's theory of sulfur and mercury. According to the *Book of Tao*, written by

the sage Lao-tzu about 550 B.C., all the energy of the Universe can be divided into the two forms of yang—which is active, masculine, fiery—and yin—which is passive, feminine, and watery. Immortality is a masculine quality, and gold and jade, which are almost pure yang, preserve bodies from corruption. "If there is gold and jade in the nine apertures of the corpse, it will preserve the body from putrefaction," wrote the alchemist Ko Hung in the 4th century A.D. Princes and lords were buried with boxes of jade for this reason.

The Chinese also related the Macrocosm of the Universe to the human body in the Microcosm of the world. For example, they identified the heart with the essence of fire, the liver with the essence of wood, the lungs with the essence of metal, the stomach with the essence of earth, and the kidneys with the essence of water.

Like Western alchemy, Chinese alchemy is filled with symbols. The following details from the *Tsan-tung-chi*, written in about the 2nd or 3rd century A.D., read like a description of the embroidered pattern on a mandarin's robe: "Cooking and distillation takes place in the cauldron; below blazes the roaring flame. Before goes the White Tiger leading the way; following comes the Gray Dragon. The fluttering Scarlet Bird flies the five colors. Encountering ensnaring nets, it is helplessly and immovably pressed down, and cries with pathos like a child after

Right: the jade funeral suit of a Chinese queen, the wife of a monarch who ruled in the late 2nd century B.C. It was believed that gold and jade, being almost purely yang, preserved the body.

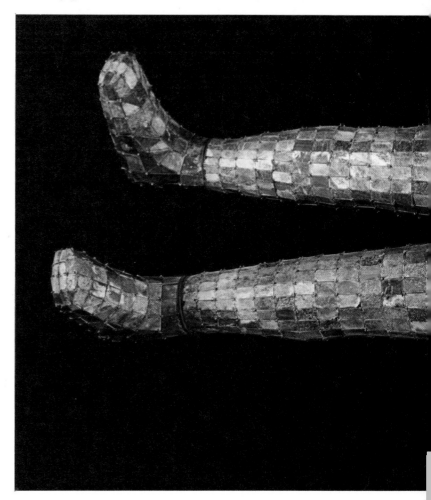

Right: Chinese alchemists in a mountain retreat. Although the Chinese were apparently originally interested in producing gold, the main—and continuing—aim of Chinese alchemy was to discover the secret of immortality. It was believed that a magic gold medicine might achieve this.

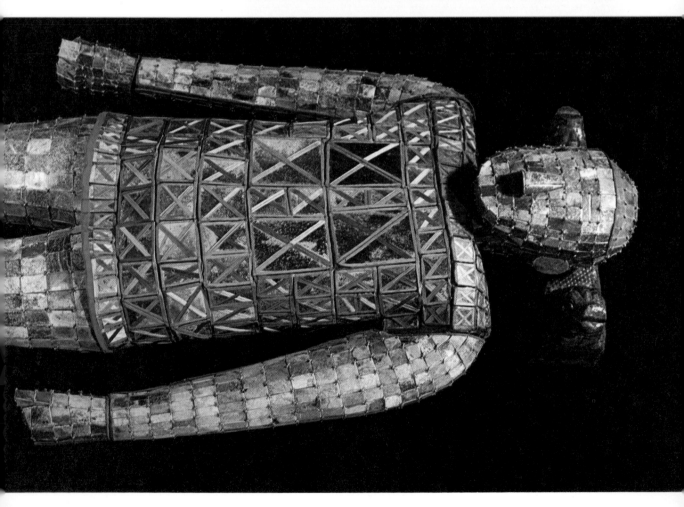

its mother. Willy-nilly it is put into the cauldron of hot fluid to the detriment of its feathers. Before half the time has passed, Dragons appear with rapidity and in great number. The five dazzling colors change incessantly. Turbulently boils the fluid in the furnace. One after another they appear to form an array as irregular as dogs' teeth. Stalagmites which are like midwinter icicles are spat out horizontally and vertically. Rocky heights of no apparent regularity make their appearance, supporting one another. When yin and yang are properly matched, tranquility prevails."

In plain words, as the English writer E. J. Holmyard has pointed out, the solution is evaporated until it crystallizes.

Of course alchemy did not just consist of theories and symbols. Jabir, for example, was capable of providing explicit descriptions of alchemical processes and apparatus. He gave the earliest known formula for the manufacture of nitric acid, and noticed that copper compounds will color a flame blue-green. He knew the use of manganese dioxide in glassmaking, he described the making of steel, dyes, and varnishes, and he reported how to make acetic acid by distilling vinegar.

Al-Razi, another great figure who lived a little later than Jabir, goes into even greater detail about the contents of the alchemist's laboratory. Al-Razi was born in about A.D. 826. The apparatus he described hardly changed within the next thousand years. In fact, although modern chemical research apparatus is highly sophisticated, most teaching laboratories are still stocked with equipment that would not have been unfamiliar to Al-Razi.

The most important part of any laboratory were the furnaces. Until the invention of the thermometer in the 18th century, it was impossible to measure heat exactly. Alchemists usually recognized four "degrees" of heat. The first degree was that of a brooding hen, or a dungheap, or the Egyptian summer; the second that of a water bath just below boiling; the third that obtained by a bath of sand or ashes placed in the furnace; and the fourth degree that of "naked heat," when the furnace was hot enough to melt metals. The sand bath and water bath are known to this day. Both are effective methods of maintaining a steady temperature.

Alchemical processes depended on the maintenance of steady temperatures, and much experience was needed in the design of furnaces to provide them with all kinds of holes that could be covered or uncovered to regulate the heat and the draft.

The Arabs were the perfecters if not the inventors of the art of distillation, in which a liquid is converted into a vapor by boiling, and then condensed back into a liquid by cooling. The aim of distillation is purification. The alchemists developed different vessels for the distillation process. The lower part of a *still*, the apparatus used for distillation, is called a *cucurbit*; the liquid is heated in this container. The upper part, where the heated vapor condenses again, is the *alembic*. The receiver for the distilled liquid is the *aludel*.

Often the liquid was *refluxed* so that after condensation in the top of the still, it ran back to be reheated without being collected in an aludel. Flasks in which this process was performed were

Above: Arab symbolic figures and diagrams of stills (on the right) from a 12th-century Arab text on alchemy. In general the Arab alchemists were less secretive about their discoveries, and the Arab manuscripts are less shrouded in complicated symbolism than the later European alchemical works.

Below: the title page of a work written by Hieronymus Brunschwig in 1507 on the art of distillation. Although European alchemists spent much time and ingenuity on the arrangement of their stills, the art was developed, if not invented, by the Arabs, and it became an enormously important process.

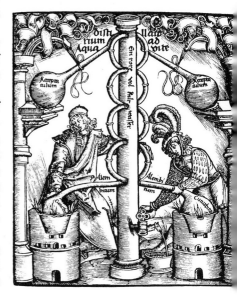

known as *pelicans* because the tube down which the refluxed liquid ran made them look something like pelicans with beaks tucked into their breasts. A special and important type of refluxing—one that is widely used in chemistry today—was employed to extract soluble material from a solid substance. The apparatus used was known as a *kerotakis*. At the bottom of the kerotakis is the furnace, which heats a liquid to boiling. The liquid vapor rises to the top of the still and condenses there, running down over the solid matter which is held in a sieve. If the solid contains anything that is even slightly soluble in the liquid, it will in the end be concentrated in the bottom of the still. Today, an apparatus of this kind is often used by analytical chemists. It is called a Soxhlet extractor.

So much for the heating of liquids. Frequently, however, it was necessary to heat substances to higher temperatures. For instance, in the calcination of metals—that is, the "burning" of them to form oxides—very strong heat is required. Similarly in the reverse process—the smelting, or "reduction" of ores to the metal—high temperatures are required. For these temperatures, a *crucible* was necessary.

The name of this apparatus, which means "little cross," describes its basic appearance. It was a small bowl, generally made of clay, with four lips extending in a cross shape so that it could be supported on the rim of a furnace. Similar was the *cupel*, a crucible made of bone ash. If gold or silver mixed with lead were heated in a cupel, the lead oxidized rapidly, the lead

Above: an Arab pharmacy from a manuscript of the 13th century. In the lower floor of the shop a pharmacist is preparing a medicine from honey. On the next level jars are stored and an assistant is checking the contents of one. The meditative figure at the upper left is the physician, who is the master of the entire pharmacy.

oxide was absorbed by the material of the cupel, and the gold or silver was left purified.

Al-Razi described much other equipment that would be familiar to any student of chemistry: beakers, flasks, crystallizing dishes, spatulas, funnels, filters made of cloth, and pestles and mortars. His shelves contained not only all the known metals, but also many other substances such as pyrites, malachite, lapis lazuli, gypsum, hematite, galena, turquoise, stibnite, alum, green vitriol, natron, borax, salt, lime, potash, cinnabar, white and red lead, iron oxide, copper oxide, vinegar, and probably caustic soda, glycerol, and sulfuric and nitric acids.

The Arabs had preserved the writings of Greek philosophers such as Aristotle, and had carried on the beliefs and practices of the early alchemists. They had also added a great deal of their own to alchemy, mainly in terms of chemical discoveries and improvements in apparatus. It was not until the 12th century, with the translations made by Robert of Chester and his followers, that medieval Europe learned of the mysterious science of alchemy.

Below left: two of the ovens used by alchemists, from Hieronymus Brunschwig's 1519 work on equipment for distilling. The upper illustration shows the ordinary oven with the distilling apparatus in the flue. Below is a type of oven in which water is heated, with four distilling vessels embedded in sand in the top of it.

Below: a German reconstruction of a 16th-century alchemical laboratory. The apparatus is neatly stored around the walls of the room, in which there are several furnaces. Judging from contemporary drawings and paintings, alchemists' workshops were seldom like this as far as tidiness is concerned.

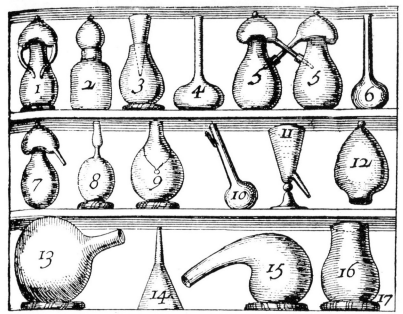

Left: apparatus that would have been used in a laboratory in the late 17th century. Although many of the vessels illustrated have since become obsolete, the following are still used in chemistry laboratories at the present time: two forms of the matrass, now called a flask, 4 and 6; the glass funnel, 14; and the retort, 16.

Two Mysterious Frenchmen

At least as late as the year 1742, there stood in the cemetery of the Holy Innocents in Paris an old arch with remarkable paintings on its walls. It had been built and decorated on the instructions of Nicholas Flamel, a man whose profession it was to copy out manuscripts and documents in the days before printing. The paintings showed the figure of Nicholas Flamel dressed as a pilgrim, strange symbolic scenes, and the various stages of a successful transmutation of ordinary metals into gold. Flamel explained the transmutation scenes as follows: "In the year of our Lord 1382, April 25, at five in the afternoon, this mercury I truly trans-

Alchemists, like alchemical texts, are often obscure and hard to understand. Medieval and modern alchemists alike seem to vanish into a tantalizing mist of theory and conjecture, with only their writings left behind—and often even the authenticity of the writings is far from certain. Above: the alchemist Nicholas Flamel, who is thought to have lived from 1330-1416, and who endowed churches, chapels, and hospitals with the alchemical gold he and his wife transmuted. Right: the seekers after material gold in the garden, one of the drawings made following Flamel's description of the illustrations in the *Book of Abraham the Jew*, which gave instructions for the transmutation. The figure at the bottom right of the picture is believed to be Flamel himself.

40

"Flamel wrote an account of his lengthy alchemical quest..."

muted into almost as much gold, much better, indeed, than common gold, more soft also, and more pliable. I may speak it with truth, I have made it three times, with the help of Perrenelle [his wife] who understood it as well as I, because she helped me in my operations . . ."

Flamel wrote an account of his lengthy alchemical quest in 1413. His devoted wife and companion, Perrenelle, had died in 1399, and for a long time he had been inconsolable. They were a thrifty, industrious, and charitable couple, and Flamel's narrative, with its sober enthusiasm, has an authentic ring. His tale begins in the year 1357 when he purchased a very old and very large gilded book. "It was not of paper, nor parchment, as other books be, but was only made of delicate rinds (as it seemed unto me) of tender young trees; the cover of it was of brass, well bound, all engraven with letters or strange figures . . . this I know that I could not read them nor were they either Latin or French letters, of which I understand something. As to the matter which was written within, it was engraved (as I suppose) with an iron pencil or graver upon the said bark leaves, done admirably well and in neat Latin letters, and curiously colored." The manuscript contained 21 leaves. The seventh, fourteenth, and twenty-first leaves were blank, apart from some strange illustrations. The seventh leaf showed "a Virgin and serpents swallowing her up," the fourteenth a cross with a serpent crucified on it, and the twenty-first "a desert with many springs out of which serpents writhed."

On the first page was written in capital letters in gold: "Abraham the Jew, Priest, Prince, Levite, Astrologer, and Philosopher, to the nation of the Jews dispersed by the wrath of God in France, wisheth health." Flamel afterward referred to the manuscript as the *Book of Abraham the Jew*. The dedication was followed by lengthy curses and execrations against anyone who might read the book who was neither a priest nor scribe. Flamel, who was a copyist or scribe, was exempt from these curses and felt emboldened to read further. On the third leaf and in all the following writings, were instructions for the transmutation of metals to gold. The author wished to help the dispersed Jews pay their taxes to the Roman Emperors. The instructions were clear and easy to follow. The only problem was that they referred to the later stages of the transmutation. There were no written instructions given as to what the *prima materia*, or first matter, consisted of, and so it seemed impossible to carry out the essential first stages of the transmutation.

The only clue the author gave to the identity of the first matter was that he had depicted it in the illustrations on the fourth and fifth leaves of the book. Flamel found to his disappointment that, although these pictures were clear and singularly well painted, "yet by that could no man ever have been able to understand it without being well skilled in their [the Hebrews'] Cabala, which is a series of old traditions, and also to have been well studied in their books." Flamel had the pictures copied and showed them to various people in the hope that someone would be able to interpret them. On one side of the fourth page was a painting of a young man with wings at his ankles. In his hand he held the *caduceus*, the snake entwined rod of Mercury, mes-

Left: an 18th-century print of the frescoes with the alchemic figures of Abraham the Jew which Flamel had erected in the cemetery of the Holy Innocents in Paris. The frescoe shows both Flamel and his wife Perrenelle kneeling.

Below: *The Last Coin*, by Steen. The Alchemist's wife sees their last coin disappear as her husband tries once again to produce gold. Perrenelle Flamel was fortunate —most alchemists' wives are shown in contemporary prints and paintings as desperately poor, surrounded by hungry children.

senger of the gods. Running and flying at him with open wings came an old man with an hourglass on his head and a scythe in his hands, as if he were about to cut off the young man's feet. On the other side of the page was a picture of a high mountain. On its summit was a blue plant with gold leaves and white and red flowers, shaking in the strong north wind, "and round about it the dragons and griffins of the north made their nest and abode."

On the first side of the fifth leaf was a rose tree in flower against the side of a hollow oak. A pure spring bubbled up at the foot of the oak and ran down through a garden to disappear into the depths. It ran through the hands of many blind people who were digging for it, but who could not recognize it except for a few who could feel its weight. On the other side of this leaf the painting showed a king with a broad sword ordering his soldiers to slaughter hundreds of babies, while their mothers flung themselves weeping at his feet. The soldiers collected the infants' blood into a bath, where the Sun and Moon came to bathe themselves.

No one who saw the pictures could understand them. At last, a man named Anselm, who was deeply interested in alchemy, claimed to be able to interpret them. Unfortunately, he started Flamel off on the wrong track. "This strange and foreign discourse to the matter was the cause of my erring, and made me wander for the space of one and twenty years in a perfect meander from the verity; in which space of time I went through a thousand labyrinths or processes, but all in vain."

Finally, Flamel's wife Perrenelle suggested that, since the manuscript came from a Jewish source, he should seek the advice of a learned Jew in interpreting it. Many Jews had at that time settled in Spain. Flamel decided to go on a pilgrimage to Saint James of Compostella, and at the same time seek help in the synagogues. Attired as a pilgrim, and carrying careful copies of the mystifying illustrations, he set off for his journey to Spain.

After he had made his devotions at the Shrine of Saint James of Compostella, Flamel tried without success to find someone who could enlighten him as to the true meaning of the pictures. He traveled on to Leon, where quite by chance he was introduced to a certain Master Canches, who was well-versed in the secrets of the Cabala and other Jewish mysteries. When he saw Flamel's copies of the illustrations he was "ravished with great astonishment and joy." He recognized them as part of a book which it was believed had been completely lost. Master Canches immediately resolved to return with Flamel to France to find out more about the manuscript. On the journey he interpreted Flamel's illustrations with such accuracy, even to the smallest detail, that Flamel was able to find out what he needed to know about the nature of the first matter. Unfortunately, Master Canches fell sick and died when they reached Orleans. Flamel buried him as well as he could afford, and sadly returned to Paris. But nothing could stifle his joy when at last he came in sight of his small house and was reunited with his wife Perrenelle. He put up a painting on the door of the chapel next to his home. It showed him kneeling with his wife and

Below: Flamel's instruments, in a miniature illustrating *Alchimie de Flamel*, a 16th-century French manuscript. The strip at the top shows the seven colors of the process, in the proper order.

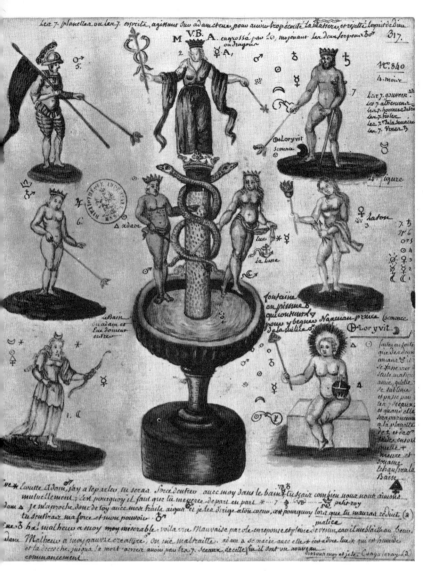

Left: the planets around the
piller of life, from the 16th-
century French manuscript. Each
stage of the process had its own
prescribed planetary situation,
a typical linking of astrology
with the alchemical tradition.

Below: the mercurial serpent is
crucified, a version of one of
the illustrations Flamel described.
It was taken to symbolize the
transformation of mercury.

giving thanks to God for granting him the desired knowledge.

However, Flamel's troubles were not yet over. "Well, I had
now the *prima materia*, the first principles, yet not their first
preparation, which is a thing most difficult, above all the things
in the world; but in the end I had that also, after long errors of
three years, or thereabouts . . . Finally, I found that which I
desired, which I also soon knew by the strong scent and odor
thereof. Having this, I easily accomplished the Mastery, for
knowing the preparation of the first Agents, and after following
my Book according to the letter, I could not have missed it
though I would. Then the first time that I made projection was
upon Mercury, whereof I turned half a pound, or thereabouts,
into pure silver, better than that of the Mine, as I myself
assayed [tested], and made others assay many times. This was
upon a Monday, the 17 of January about noon, in my home,
Perrenelle only being present, in the year of the restoring of
mankind 1382."

Three months later, Flamel made his first transmutation into
gold. For a long time he was worried that Perrenelle, who was
overjoyed at the final outcome of so many years of experiments,

would let some word slip among her family and reveal the secret of their sudden wealth. "But the goodness of the most great God had not only given and filled me with this blessing, to give me a chaste and sober wife, but she was also a wise and prudent woman, not only capable of reason but also to do what was reasonable, and was more discreet and secret than ordinarily other women are."

Because she was now well past the age for bearing children, Perrenelle suggested that their riches should be devoted to charity. She and Flamel founded and endowed "fourteen hospitals, three chapels, and seven churches, in the city of Paris, all which we had new built from the ground, and enriched with great gifts and revenues, with many reparations in their church-yards. We also have done at Boulogne about as much as we have done at Paris, not to speak of the charitable acts which we both did to particular poor people, principally to widows and orphans . . ."

The arch built by Flamel in the cemetery of the Holy Inno-cents, with its strange alchemical paintings, disappeared some time in the 18th century. The painting of Flamel and his wife giving thanks to God on the door of the chapel next to their home has also vanished. But one day in the mid-19th century, a herbalist in one of the streets near where Flamel used to live turned over the finely polished marble slab on which he had for years been chopping his dried herbs, and found it to be Flamel's tombstone. It is now preserved in the Museum of Cluny in Paris, and the inscription reads: "Nicholas Flamel, formerly a scrivener, left in his will for the administration of this church certain rents and houses which he acquired and bought during his lifetime to provide for masses and distribution of alms each year, in particular the Quinze-Vingts [a hospital in Paris for blind men] cathedral and other churches and hospitals of Paris." The will of Perrenelle, dated 1399, survives, and so does Flamel's, which he signed on November 22, 1416. Three years later he died.

After Flamel's death, many people thought that some of the Philosopher's Stone must still be hidden in one of his houses. His property was searched over and over again, and so thorough-ly that one house was reduced to a pile of rubble with only the cellars remaining. By about 1560 the local magistrate, in the name of the king, took possession of all property that had once belonged to Flamel, so that a final thorough search could be made. But nobody ever admitted to having found anything.

There were those, of course, who insisted that Flamel, having discovered the secret of the Philosopher's Stone, had also dis-covered the secret of immortality. The 17th-century traveler Paul Lucas, during a discussion on alchemy and magic with a Turkish philosopher from Asia Minor, was told, "that true philosophers had the secret of prolonging life for anything up to a thousand years."

"At last I took the liberty of naming the celebrated Flamel, who, it was said, possessed the Philosopher's Stone, yet was certainly dead. He smiled at my simplicity, and asked with an air of mirth: 'Do you really believe this? No, no, my friend, Flamel is still living; neither he nor his wife has yet tasted death.

Above: Flamel's tombstone, one of the few indisputable relics left of his historical reality. The upper portion shows carved repre-sentations of Christ, Saint Peter, and Saint Paul, and between them the symbols of gold (or the sun) and silver (or the moon), but the inscription makes no mention of his alchemical achievements. Below: the church of Saint-Jacques -la-Boucherie where Flamel was buried. The church was demolished in the late 18th century, with only the tower, now used as a meteorological station, remaining.

Left: a reconstruction of Flamel's house in Paris. Across the front was a frieze that showed Flamel and his wife in prayer, surrounded by various alchemical figures.

It was probably to this house that King Charles VI of France sent his minister to investigate rumors that Flamel was a successful alchemist. The minister visited the pair, but observing that they ate off earthenware platters, decided that the tales of Flamel's alchemy were obviously pure invention, and reported so to his king.

Below: Flamel's house in 1900.

Above: this figure described by Flamel has been interpreted as signifying the fixing of mercury. The old man with the scythe, symbolizing lead, cuts off the feet of Mercury and renders ordinary quicksilver, regarded as a baser, immobile form of silver. Right: another of the figures is called The Three Colors of the Work. The first rider, mounted on a black lion, symbolizes gold in maceration; the second, on the red lion, shows the inner ferment; and the crowned rider on the white lion symbolizes final success.

It is not above three years since I left both the one and the other in India; he is one of my best friends.'"

According to the Turk, Flamel had realized the danger he was in if ever the news got out that he possessed the Philosopher's Stone. Perrenelle had therefore feigned illness and had gone to Switzerland, leaving Nicholas to announce her death. He buried a log in her grave. After several years he in his turn carried out the same deception. Nearly a century later, in 1761, Flamel and his wife were reported to have attended a performance of the opera in Paris, and there were many other stories of a similar nature.

One of the most detailed and most fantastic of such tales appears in the little-known work of *Le Corbeau Menteur* (The

Lying Raven) by the 19th-century French writer Ninian Bres. He
wrote: "He was a little less than middle height, stooping somewhat with the weight of years, but still with a firm step and a
clear eye, and with a complexion strangely smooth and almost
transparent, like fine alabaster. Both he and the woman with
him—clearly his wife, although she appeared almost imper-
ceptibly the older and more decisive of the two—were dressed
in a style that seemed only a few years out of fashion and yet
had an indefinable air of antiquity about it. I stood, half concealed in a little archway toward the end of the boulevard du
Temple: my hands were stained with acid, and my topcoat
stank of the furnace. As the couple came abreast of the spot
where I stood, Flamel turned toward me and seemed about to

Above: a bas relief on the Great Porch of the cathedral of Notre Dame, Paris, which depicts alchemy. The mysterious French alchemist Fulcanelli claimed that all the secrets of alchemy can be found in the carvings of the Great Porch of Notre-Dame.

Right: Notre-Dame Cathedral. It has long been claimed that the Gothic cathedrals in France were secret textbooks of hidden wisdom; using complicated linguistic arguments, Fulcanelli declared that the secrets were those of alchemy, awaiting a student capable of understanding them.

speak, but Perrenelle drew him quickly on, and they were almost at once lost in the crowd. You ask how I am so confident that this was Nicholas Flamel? I tell you that I have spent many hours in the Bibliothèque Nationale, poring over the *Figures d'Abraham Juif* [*Pictures of Abraham the Jew*]: look carefully at the first side of the fifth leaf and there, in the lower right-hand corner of the representation of those who seek for gold in the garden, you will see the face that searched mine that evening of the boulevard du Temple, and that has haunted my dreams ever since."

The illustration to which Bres refers is from a manuscript previously thought to be of Flamel's day but now considered to be of the 17th century. It is only one of many different attempts to reproduce the book that Flamel described so carefully. In different but obviously similar forms these pictures have appeared over and over again in alchemical works through the centuries. The manuscript also attempts an explanation of the meaning of the illustrations that puzzled Flamel for so long, and this interpretation has been expanded by numerous later writers. For example, take the illustration of the young man with wings on his ankles being attacked by an old man with a scythe. The first stage in the explanation was that these two figures stood for Mercury and Saturn. The second stage was that Mercury, in alchemical terms, represented an impure form of silver, and Saturn meant lead. When imperfect silver and lead are heated together in a cupel, the impurities of the silver are absorbed into the material of the crucible, and the resulting silver is said to be "fixed" in the sense of stable or permanent. This illustration, represented in symbolic terms, is the alchemical process necessary for the fixing of silver.

From the time of Flamel on, alchemy became increasingly symbolical. The mysterious 20th-century alchemist Fulcanelli, in fact, suggested that the whole of Flamel's story was pure symbolism. He wrote: "We are prepared to certify—if our sincerity is to be trusted—that Flamel never quitted the cellar where his furnaces roared. Anyone who knows the significance of the pilgrim's staff, the begging bowl and the cockleshell in Saint James' hat will also know that we are speaking the truth. By substituting himself for the material and modeling himself upon other secret workers, the great Adept was obeying the rules of philosophic discipline and following the example of his predecessors."

The true identity of Fulcanelli himself is uncertain. He is best known as the alleged author of a book in French, *The Mystery of the Cathedrals.* In this he claims to show that all the secrets of alchemy are concealed in the carvings of the central porch of Notre Dame and various of the porches of the cathedral in Amiens. Fulcanelli proposes that gothic art, *l'art goth*, of which the French cathedrals are outstanding examples, is really *argot*, the language of the common people. They in turn are descendants of those intrepid adventurers who sought the Golden Fleece, the sailors aboard the *Argo*. In all this he claims to discover what he has called "the phonetic Cabala."

One example must suffice. In writing of the labyrinth, Fulcanelli refers to the thread of Ariadne in the Greek myth. Ariadne is Ariane in French. "Ariane is a forme of *airagne* (*araignée*, the spider) by metathesis [transposition] of the i," he said. ". . . Is not our soul the spider, which weaves our own body? But this word appears in other forms. The verb *airo* (Greek) means to take, to seize, to draw, to attract; whence *airen*, that which takes, seizes, attracts. Thus *airen* is the lodestone, that virtue shut up in the body, which the wise call their Magnesia . . . In Provençal iron is called aran and iran, according to the different dialects. This is the masonic Hiram, the divine ram, the architect of the Temple of Solomon . . . Compare all that with the Greek *Sideros*, which may mean either iron or lodestone. Nor is this all. The verb *aruo* means the rising star from out of the sea, whence *aryan*, the star which rises out of the sea; our *ariane* is thus the Orient, by the permutation of vowels. Further *arua* has also the sense to attract; thus *aryan* is also the lodestone. If we now compare *Sideros*, which has given the Latin *sidus*, *sideris*, a star, we shall recognize our Provençal aran, iran, airan—the Greek *aryan*, the rising sun."

Is this genuine, or is it some heavy-handed hoax? Scholars have argued for and against the existence of Fulcanelli ever since the publication of his book in 1925. In his preface to the first edition, Eugene Canseliet, a well-known writer on alchemy, wrote: "For a long time now the author of this book has not been among us . . . My Master . . . disappeared when the fatal hour struck, when the Sign was accomplished . . . Fulcanelli is no more." Then in March 1953 the French writer Louis Pauwels met an alchemist in the Café Procope in Paris. "How old can he be? He says 35. That seems surprising. He has white curly hair, trimmed so as to look like a wig. Lots of deep wrinkles in a pink skin and full features. Few gestures, but slow,

Above: Louis Pauwels, the French writer, photographed in 1974. Twenty-one years earlier Pauwels had a strange encounter with a mysterious alchemist in a Parisian *café*. The alchemist, who seemed to belong to another age, implied that Fulcanelli was not dead, as his student, Eugene Canseliet, apparently suggested in his preface to Fulcanelli's *The Mystery of the Cathedrals*. Pauwels came to believe that the alchemist he had met was Fulcanelli himself.

calculated and effective when he does make them. A calm, keen smile; eyes that laugh, but in a detached sort of way. Everything about him suggests another age . . . I asked him about Fulcanelli, and he gave me to understand that Fulcanelli is not dead . . ."

A few weeks later Pauwels met Jacques Bergier, a scientist, with whom he later collaborated in writing on the occult. Bergier told Pauwels of his own meeting with a man whom he guessed to be Fulcanelli. It happened one afternoon in June 1937. Bergier said that he met the alchemist by appointment in a laboratory of the Gas Board in Paris. Bergier at that time was working as research assistant to André Helbronner, the French atomic physicist. Fulcanelli (if it was he) told Bergier: "You are on the brink of success, as indeed are several other of our scientists today. May I be allowed to warn you to be careful? . . . The liberation of atomic energy is easier than you think, and the radioactivity artificially produced can poison the atmosphere of our planet in the space of a few years. Moreover, atomic explosives can be produced from a few grains of metal powerful enough to destroy whole cities. I am telling you this for a fact: the alchemists have known it for a very long time . . .

"I shall not attempt to prove to you what I am now going to say, but I ask you to repeat it to M. Helbronner: certain geometrical arrangements of highly purified materials are enough to release atomic forces without having recourse to either electricity or vacuum techniques . . . The secret of alchemy is this: there is a way of manipulating matter and energy so as to produce what modern scientists call a *field of force*. This field acts on the observer and puts him in a privileged position vis-à-vis the Universe. From this position he has access to the realities which are ordinarily hidden from us by time and space, matter and energy. This is what we call the Great Work."

In an introduction to the English edition of *The Mystery of the Cathedrals* Walter Lang carries the Fulcanelli legend further, reporting that "after a lapse of many years, Canseliet received a message from the alchemist and met him at a prearranged rendezvous. The reunion was brief, for Fulcanelli once again severed contact and once again disappeared without leaving a trace of his whereabouts." But, says Lang, Fulcanelli had grown younger, for whereas he had been an old man of 80 when Canseliet had first met him, 30 years later he appeared to be a man of 50.

Says Louis Pauwels: "All that we know of him is that he survived the war and disappeared completely after the Liberation. Every attempt to find him failed." It is difficult to decide how deliberate these attempts to find Fulcanelli were. In August 1945 the American intelligence services asked Bergier to contact urgently a certain anonymous major who worked for an organization searching out German research reports on atomic energy. This major desperately wanted to know the whereabouts of Fulcanelli—but he appears to have been satisfied when Bergier assured him that the veteran alchemist had once more disappeared. After 50 years, we know no more of Fulcanelli now than we knew in 1925. Perhaps, with Nicholas Flamel, he lives the life of an Indian Mahatma in the distant hills. Perhaps, who knows, he *is* Nicholas Flamel.

Below: André Helbronner, noted French atomic physicist. His research assistant, Jacques Bergier, was approached by a mysterious stranger in 1937, who warned him that science was on the brink of manipulating nuclear energy, and that in the past this same abyss had been crossed with disastrous consequences. The stranger asked Bergier to convey the warning to Helbronner. Bergier was convinced that the stranger was Fulcanelli. Helbronner was later killed by the Nazis during World War II.

4

The Medieval Masters

Maybe the newly appointed city physician had been drinking too much. He usually had. "Always drunk and always lucid," someone has described him. He stood in the city square of Basel, Switzerland, with a large brass pan in which charcoal was burning. In one hand he held a book of the works of Avicenna, and in the other the works of Galen. Then he thrust them into the flames and sprinkled them with sulfur and saltpeter so that they burned with an unearthly light. "If your physicians," he said "only knew that their prince Galen—they call none like him—was sticking in hell, from whence he has sent letters to me, they would

The alchemists of the medieval period were a fascinating and enigmatic group of individuals. Most often the facts and legends that have survived the centuries tantalize us with the half-hidden glimpses of extraordinary men who single-mindedly pursued the mystical goal of transmutation. Right: an Alchemist from *Splendor Solis*, a manuscript reputedly written by the most mysterious medieval alchemist, who is known to us now only by his pseudonym, Solomon Trismosin. Nothing but what he wrote of himself has survived—but if he wrote the truth, he succeeded in finding both the Philosopher's Stone and the coveted Elixir of Life.

55

"Paracelsus... was not a man given to modesty"

make the sign of the cross upon themselves with a fox's tail. In the same way your Avicenna sits in the vestibule of the infernal portal . . ."

At that time, in the 16th century, medical knowledge was based almost exclusively on the writings of Galen, a Greek physician of the 2nd century A.D., and Avicenna, the Arab philosopher who died in 1037. It was unheard of to question their authority, let alone to claim to know better. Yet here was someone not only insulting these masters, but also all the doctors who followed their teachings. "Come then, and listen, impostors who prevail only by the authority of your high positions!" the scoffer continued. "After my death, my disciples will burst forth and drag you to the light, and shall expose your dirty drugs . . ." and so on. The speech of this overwhelmingly self-confident man could truly be called *bombastic*—and that was his name—Philippus Aureolus Theophrastus Bombastus von Hohenheim. But he is known to generations of alchemists as Paracelsus, the name he gave himself to indicate that he was greater (*para* is Greek for beyond) than Celsus, the Roman medical authority of the beginning of the Christian era.

Paracelsus was born on December 17, 1493 near Zurich, the son of a local physician. His father taught him the rudiments of alchemy, astrology, and medicine as soon as he was old enough to understand. At 16 Paracelsus entered the university in Basel, and later he probably went to Würzburg to study under Hans von Trittenheim, a celebrated expert on magic. When he was 22 he worked for a year at the mining school of Sigismund Fugger, who was renowned as an alchemist. But this was far from being the completion of Paracelsus' education. He next set out on an odyssey that probably went through Germany, Italy, France, the Netherlands, England, Scandinavia, and Russia. In Italy he served as an army surgeon, and took a degree in medicine at the university of Ferrara. At the age of 33 he was invited to Basel in his native Switzerland to take up the post of town physician and professor of medicine.

Although Paracelsus performed some marvelous cures in Basel, he soon made enemies. One day, for example, he invited all the doctors to a lecture in which he proposed to teach them some of his greatest secrets. When he began by uncovering a dish full of dung, they left the hall in a hurry. Paracelsus boomed after them: "If you will not learn the mysteries of putrefactive fermentation, you are unworthy of the name of physicians."

It was not long before Paracelsus had quarreled bitterly with the city authorities, and was on the road again. For most of the rest of his life he wandered around, writing as he traveled in a strange mixture of German, Latin, and words that he made up himself. Capriciously, he took the Arabic word for black eye-paint, *al-kohl*, and gave it to spirits of wine, which has borne the name alcohol ever since. He invented the name zinc. From the German *all-geist* he derived the word *alkahest*, the imaginary universal solvent with the power to convert all bodies into their liquid primary matter. For his own kind of alchemy, which was concerned with healing, he coined the word "spagyric."

Paracelsus' main aim in alchemy was to use its methods to prepare medicines. Although he did not deny the possibility of

Above: this drawing, a *Young Man with a Broad-brimmed Hat*, is frequently assumed to be a portrait of the young Paracelsus. Right: *The Apothecary, late 16th Century*, by H. Stacey Marks. Apothecaries relied on herbs for their medicines, and persecuted Paracelsus when he began to develope medicines based on chemical substances. Their enmity helped drive Paracelsus on his wanderings in other countries, where he spread medical alchemy. Below: the title page of Hieronymus Brunschwig's 1519 work on distillation. The techniques of distillation were used not only for alchemical work, but also for the widely used herbal medicines.

Right: the 24th Figure of the 32 allegorical prophecies of Paracelsus, first published in 1530. The text accompanying this one said in part "Ye should not be as beasts but as men, but as ye are not so, he will rule you that is above you, of whome stands written; give unto him what to him belongs." Paracelsus' "elucidation" says, "Therefore also alliances must be dissolved that were only made to cause discord and to accomplish the heart's desire."

58

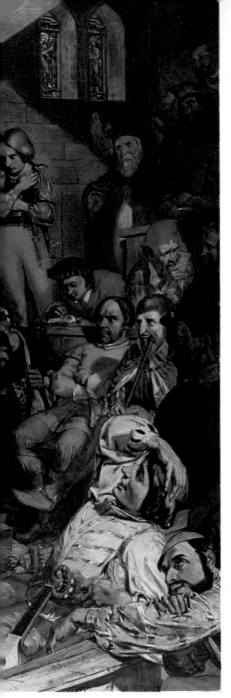

making gold, it was of little importance to him. "Men have said of alchemy," he wrote, "that it is for the making of gold and silver. For me such is not the aim, but to consider only that virtue and power may lie in medicines." At that time doctors used herbal remedies almost exclusively. Paracelsus' introduction of medicines based on chemical substances was revolutionary, and its effects were far-reaching. Inspired by his work in alchemy, a whole new school of medical chemistry sprang up. This school united the discoveries of medicine with those of alchemy.

Paracelsus heaped abuse on most of the doctors of his time. He was warm in his praise, however, for those few physicians who had studied alchemy and knew how to apply their knowledge. "They are sooty and dirty like the smiths and charcoal-burners," he said, "and hence make little show, make not many words and gossip with their patients, do not highly praise their own remedies, for they well know that the work must praise the master, not the master his work. . . . Therefore they let such things alone and busy themselves with working with their fires and learning the steps of alchemy."

The bombastic doctor seems to have been responsible for diverting the course of alchemy away from transmutation of metals. Some practitioners, under his guidance, used alchemical processes to find medical cures. Others turned to mystic contemplation. Paracelsus believed that the gold that could be made by transmutation was poor and unproductive in comparison with the "gold" that could be produced by exercising the secret powers existing in the soul. Many alchemists, influenced by Paracelsus, abandoned the physical search for gold, and began to look within themselves for secret strength.

Paracelsus believed that the material world was ultimately composed of the four Aristotelian elements of Earth, Air, Fire, and Water, but that more immediately it was made up of three substances. These were known as mercury, sulfur, and salt, and were sometimes referred to as the *tria prima.* They were not the actual substances that we know by these names today, but stood for certain principles. Mercury, also known as the spirit, stood for the principles of fusibility and volatility. Sulfur, which represented the soul, stood for inflammability, and salt, the body, stood for incombustibility and nonvolatility. In this theory Paracelsus had revived an old Arabic idea that metals were formed from a combination of sulfur and mercury. He added the third principle of salt, and extended the definition to include all material substances.

"As many as there are kinds of fruit, so many kinds there are of sulfur, salt, and so many of mercury. A different sulfur is in gold, another in silver, another in lead, another in iron, tin, etc. Also a different one in sapphire, another in the emerald, another in the ruby, chrysolite, amethyst, magnets, etc. Also another in stones, flint, salts, springwaters, etc. And not only so many kinds of sulfur but also as many kinds of salt, different ones in metals, different ones in gems, stones, others in salts, in vitriol, in alum. Similarly with mercuries, a different one in the metals, another in gems, and as often as there is a species there is a different mercury. . . . And further they are still more divided, as

there is not merely one kind of gold but many kinds of gold. . . . Therefore there are just as many kinds of sulfurs of gold, salts of gold, mercuries of gold."

This kind of philosophy, emanating from someone with as strong a personality as Paracelsus, had an immeasurable influence on the theories of the alchemists. In the sense that it made all practical work much more difficult to conceive, it is certainly true that Paracelsus' doctrine encouraged a more mystic approach to alchemy. So, on the one hand, he was claimed by those looking to alchemy for medical cures as the father of medical chemistry. On the other hand, he was regarded by those turning from practical experiments in transmutation to contemplation as the founder of mystic alchemy.

Paracelsus was not the only physician of this time to be subsequently claimed by both scientists and magicians as a major influence. Henry Cornelius Agrippa of Nettesheim was another. His whole career, in fact, was very like that of his contemporary Paracelsus, who was only seven years older than he. Agrippa served as a soldier in Germany, traveled through France, Spain, Italy, England, and Switzerland, and during his short life was a professor, courtier, theologian, lawyer, doctor, and alchemist. He died at the age of 49.

Agrippa's philosophy was expressed at length in his famous work on magic, *The Occult Philosophy*, which he probably wrote in 1510 during a visit to England. It is based on the idea that "man is made in the image of God." God is seen as consisting of the whole Universe, and therefore man is the miniature replica of the Universe. Just as man's body contains his spirit, so all material substances are permeated by a Universal Spirit. This spirit was especially abundant in the various celestial bodies, and fell to earth in the rays of the stars. It was widely held at the time that various substances such as gems, metals, plants, and animals were under the influence of a particular planet or star. Agrippa believed that they were also particularly imbued with the spirit from that star. He strongly advocated charms of all kinds, which could be "worn on the body bound to any part of it or hung round the neck, changing sickness into health or health into sickness. . . . When any star ascends fortunately take a herb and stone that are under that star, make a ring of the metal that is congruous therewith, and in that fix the stone with the herb under it."

It was only a short step from this belief to the belief that it was possible to extract this spirit from the metal that was under a particular star, and project it upon another metal—if possible, under the influence of that same star. In this way the quintessence of gold might be removed from gold and projected upon lead to turn the lead into gold. But Agrippa realized that this method was unlikely to result in the multiplication of gold. In 1526 he wrote cynically to a friend: "Blessed be the Lord, I am a rich man, if there be truth in fable. A man of considerations . . . has brought me seeds of gold and planted them over my furnace within long-necked flasks, putting underneath a little fire as of the Sun's heat, and as hens brood over eggs we keep the warmth up night and day, expecting forthwith to produce enormous golden chicks. If all be hatched we shall exceed Midas in

Left: Henry Cornelius Agrippa, after a drawing by Theodore de Bry. Agrippa was a flamboyant character, not unlike Paracelsus in personality. Both men were interested in the mysticism behind alchemy, both men were fatally incapable of keeping their mouths shut—and consequently both were continually in trouble with those they had insulted or offended. Below: an alchemist at work, an engraving taken from the 1558 painting by Pieter Brueghel the Elder. Agrippa became sufficiently disillusioned with alchemy and alchemists to write bleakly of alchemists very much like the one Brueghel pictured: stubbornly pursuing his research while his wife and children starved, and eventually being led off to the poorhouse, all his money spent.

wealth, or at least in length of ears . . . ."—that is, in stupidity.

Agrippa continued his alchemical studies for many years, but final disillusionment led him to attack not only the physicians and apothecaries of his time, but the alchemists as well. In *The Vanity of Sciences and Arts*, published in 1531, he said:

"The alchemist may earn a scanty livelihood by the production of medicaments or cosmetics, or he may use his art, as very many do, to carry on the business of a coiner. But the true searcher after the Stone which is to metamorphose all base metals into gold, converts only farms, goods and patrimonies into ashes and smoke." He added somewhat grudgingly, "Nevertheless, I do not deny that to this art many excellent inventions owe their origin. Hence we have the discovery of azure, cinnabar, minium, purple, that which is called musical gold, and other colors. Hence we derive the knowledge of brass and mixed metals, solders, tests and precipitants."

Contemporary with Paracelsus and Agrippa there lived a third alchemist who, if the story is to be believed, succeeded in preparing a tincture that was the Philosopher's Stone. When one part of this tincture was added to 1500 parts of silver, it turned it all to gold. We do not know this alchemist's real name, but he

wrote under the pseudonym of Solomon Trismosin. One of his works, *Aureum Vellus*, sometimes translated as *The Golden Fleece*, was published in 1598.

According to the preface to *Aureum Vellus*, Trismosin set out on his wanderings in 1473. The first alchemist he came across was a miner named Flocker, but he was extremely secretive and Trismosin learned nothing from him. "He used a process with common lead," Trismosin recounts, "adding to it a peculiar Sulfur, or Brimstone, he fixed the lead until it became hard, then fluid, and later on soft like Wax. Of this prepared lead he took 20 loth [10 ounces], and 1 mark [about 8 ounces] pure unalloyed silver, cast it in an ingot, when half of it was gold. . . . Shortly thereafter he tumbled down a mine and no one could tell what was the artifice he had used."

In the course of the next 18 months' travel, Trismosin observed all kinds of alchemical operations "of no great importance," although he claimed that he had seen "the reality of some of the *particular* processes," and spent a good sum of his own money. In Italy he worked with a tradesman who made English tin look like the best silver, and sold it as such. Trismosin took some of this silvered tin to Venice to have it professionally analyzed, but though it looked convincing, it did not stand up to the test.

One of the assistants who had helped test the metal was curious to know how Trismosin had come by it. Trismosin offered to show him the secret, and they struck up an acquaintance. When the assistant found that Trismosin was traveling in order to gain experience of working in alchemical laboratories, he told him of an Italian nobleman who had just such a laboratory, and who was in need of some help. He introduced Trismosin to the nobleman's chief chemist, who took him to a large mansion some miles outside Venice. "I never saw such laboratory work, in all kinds of Particular Processes, and medicines, as in that place," said Trismosin. "There everything one could think of was provided and ready for use. Each workman had his own private room, and there was a special cook for the whole staff of laboratory assistants."

As a test the chief chemist gave him some metal to work on. It was cinnabar, which he had covered with all kinds of dirt in order to find out how much Trismosin knew. He had two days in which to turn it to gold. "I was kept busy, but succeeded with the Particular Process, and on testing the ingot of the fixed Mercury, the whole weighed nine loth, the test gave three loth of fine Gold. That was my first work and stroke of luck. The Chief Chemist reported it to the nobleman, who came out unexpectedly, spoke to me in Latin, called me his Fortunatum, tapped me on the shoulder and gave me 29 crowns."

Trismosin reported that this nobleman had spent some 30,000 crowns on his experiments. "I myself witnessed that he paid 6000 crowns for the manuscript *Sarlamethon*, a process for a Tincture in the Greek language. . . . I brought that process to a finish in 15 weeks. Therewith I tinged three metals into fine Gold."

Unhappily, the nobleman was drowned in a storm in the Adriatic, and the laboratory was shut up and the men paid off.

Right: Introduction of the Great Work, from the manuscript *Splendor Solis* by Solomon Trismosin. The picture is symbolic of the first stages of the process. The man on the left is the alchemist, being introduced by the philosopher to the living tree. Mercury is the man in black taking a branch. The tree emerges from the *materia confusa*, the ordinary stuff that the alchemist will have to work into gold. The crown around it signifies that it will be transformed. The birds represent the results of the first calcination, in which material is burned black and then turns into white, which in actuality is the ash.

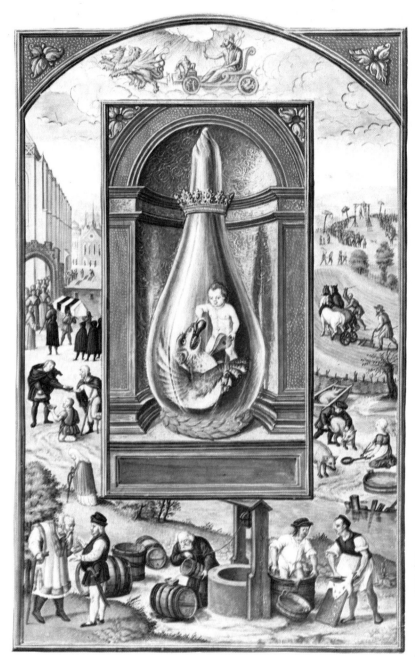

Three stages of the Great Work—the creation of the Philosopher's Stone—from *Splendor Solis*. Left: the boy, probably Mercurius as the midget, is pouring liquid on the dragon and puffing as this earthy matter is inflamed and heated during the process of calcination, during which it is burned down into ashes. Below: the three birds, red, white, and black, within the alembic symbolize the matter that is heated up into elements which are separate. They separate only to reunite, and the three birds recombine in the next stage into a superior single bird created from the materials of the three.

Trismosin describes how he then moved on "to a still better place for my purpose, where Cabalistic and Magical books in Egyptian language were entrusted to my care, these I had carefully translated into Greek, and then again retranslated into Latin. There I found and captured the Treasure of the Egyptians. I also saw what was the great Subject they worked with . . . After a while I saw the fundamental principles of this art, then I began working out the Best Tincture (but they all proceed, in the most indescribable manner, from the same root)."

Alchemists could judge whether or not their work was progressing successfully by certain color changes that occurred at the end of each stage. The first stage led to a process of rotting or putrefaction in which the material was reduced to first matter. This was known as the *nigredo* or black stage. Following this the material was reborn, the color gradually lightened, and

64

**Above: a late stage in the Great Work. The peacock symbolizes the rainbow colors that would appear to reassure the adept that he was on the right path. Alchemists believed that there was a definite sequence of colors during the progress of the Work, and if the wrong color occurred at the wrong time, it indicated sure failure.
It was often recorded that as the colors of the peacock's tail appeared in the Philosopher's Egg, a wonderful scent also came forth.**

at a certain point there would be a multitude of colors. The next color change was to white, the *albedo* stage. Then the material would pass through a yellow stage to the final one, the *rubedo* or red stage. This red tincture was the miraculous Philosopher's Stone that could turn metals to gold. Trismosin describes this stage as follows: "When I came to the end of the work I found such a beautiful red color as no scarlet can compare with, and such treasure as words cannot tell, and which can be infinitely augmented."

This translation of Solomon Trismosin's life story was made in 1921 by a certain J.K., whose true identity remains unknown. J.K. also added a summary in his own words of how he interpreted Trismosin's description of "the alchemical process called the 'Red Lion.'" The following, in which J.K. makes comments in parenthesis, is his summary:

"1. Take 4 ounces calcined alum, 4 ounces calcined saltpeter, and 2 ounces calcined sublimate, and sublimate [refine] in a proper subliming vessel.

2. Carefully take out the sublimate, and resublimate it with 10 ounces fresh salts. During this operation it will be wholesome, on account of the poisonous fumes, to eat bread thickly spread with butter.

3. Put the sublimate in a glass retort, and cover it with alcohol, and distill it over in water bath until half the fluid remains as an oil behind.

4. The alcohol distilled over is poured back (cohobated) on the residue in the retort, until it is covered about a finger's breadth.

5. This distillation repeat three times, and the whole of the sublimate will pass over into the recipient. This is the Mercury of the Philosophers, the Mercurial Water, as it were "the Hellish fire in water." This Mercurial Water fumes always, and must be kept in a closed phial, or glass-stoppered bottle.

6. Take fine gold, in leaf or thin beaten, put it in a glass retort, just cover it with the Mercurial Water, and put the retort on gentle heat, when the Water will begin to act upon the gold, and dissolve it, but it will not be reduced to a liquid entirely, and only remain at the bottom like a greasy substance, then pour off the Mercurial Water, which can be used again.

7. The gold sediment divide into two parts. Take one half and pour thereon alcohol, and let the mixture putrefy on gentle heat fifteen days, and it will become blood red; this is the *Lion's Blood*.

8. This Lion's Blood pour into another glass retort, or phial, which seal hermetically, and give it the heat of the Dog Days, and it will at first turn black, then variegated, then light gray; when heat is increased it will turn yellow and at last deep red. This is the first Tincture. (Provided it does not explode!)

9. The Red Tincture triturate (How will a fulminate triturate?) in a glass mortar. Take one grain thereof, wrap it in paper and project it on 1000 grains of gold in fusion. When it has remained in fusion for ¾ hour, the gold will turn to the second Tincture.

10. Take one part of this Tincture, project it on one thousand parts fine silver, and it will transmute it into fine gold.

11. Project one part of the first Tincture, wrapped in paper, upon 1000 parts of pure quicksilver, which has been heated until

Right: a section of the first *Ripley Scrowle*, produced in Lübeck in 1589, part of the papers of the English alchemist George Ripley. At the top are shown the seven processes of the alchemist, who is portrayed as a monk. Each is linked to the whole Work, shown as a red essence of the Stone. At the bottom a women embraces a man, symbolizing the union of the male and female (in alchemical terms, opposites). The man is rising out of the fountain where the Tree of Life grows inside the Fortress. The figures on the Fortress walls are alchemists. Beneath them, a dragon threatens a toad, which was Ripley's symbol for the important *materia prima*.

the fumes arise, and the quicksilver will be changed into the third Tincture.

12. Take one part of this Tincture, wrapped in paper, project the same on 1000 parts heated quicksilver, and it will become transmuted into fine gold.

13. Take one part of the second Tincture, and project it on copper in fusion, and it will be transmuted into gold of a very red color.

14. Project some of the second Tincture on red hot iron, insert the iron again into the blaze, and it will be transmuted into brittle gold.

15. Melt the gold that has been transmuted of the iron, with equal gold that has been transmuted from quicksilver, and it will become good malleable gold.

16. Dissolve some of the second Tincture in strong alcoholic wine, and take a spoonful in the morning. It will strengthen and renew your constitution. It rejuvenates the aged and makes women prolific."

These instructions may be impossible to follow, especially since the unstable substance formed at one stage is, J.K. suggests, the mercury fulminate used in percussion caps. But they are at least clear and couched in ordinary language. Most alchemical writings concealed their true meanings in a wealth of obscure symbols and doubletalk, as in the *Vision* of George Ripley. Ripley was born early in the 15th century in Yorkshire, England, and died at a Carmelite monastery in Lincolnshire in 1490. He was reportedly an accomplished alchemist and wrote a number of works. His *Compound of Alchimie* was written in 1471, and was dedicated to King Edward IV. But his most famous composition was his *Vision*, a poem that was copied in many different manuscripts, and was reprinted several times.

Ripley describes how, when he was reading late one night, he had a strange vision of a toad who drank the juice of grapes so quickly that its body become bloated and poisoned.
"A toade full rudde I saw did drink the juice of grapes so fast,
Till over charged with the broth, his bowels all to brast;
And after that from poysoned bulke he cast his venom fell."
The toad returned to his "secret den," exuding venom.
"His cave with blasts of fumous ayre he all be-whyted then;
And from the which in space a golden humor did ensue,
Whose falling drops from high did stain the soile with ruddy
    hew;"
As the toad began to die it turned coal black in color. Decaying in its own poison, it stood rotting for 84 days. Then Ripley put the carcass over a gentle heat in order to expel the remainder of the venom. When this had been done, a wonderful transformation took place.
"The toade with Colors rare through every side was pearst,
And White appeared when all the sundry hewes were past,
Which after being tincted Rudde, for evermore did last.
Then of the venome handled thus a medicine I did make,
Which venome kills and saveth such as venome chance to take.
Glory be to Him the graunter of such secret wayes,
Dominion, and Honor, both with Worship and with Prayes."

If we look carefully at the poem it gradually becomes clear

Above: a 16th-century engraving of the green lion devouring the sun. In the complicated alchemical symbolism, this can be translated as meaning that *aqua regia* (royal water)—a mixture of nitric and hydrochloric acids—dissolved gold, represented by the sun. The gold often contained some copper, which would color the acid bluish-green, and this explains the color of the lion. The engraving can therefore be seen as a vivid description of a straightforward chemical process.

that Ripley is not describing the death and decay of a drunken toad, but is using complex symbolism to describe the alchemical process. The color changes of alchemy are set down clearly in the correct order. First there is the black stage of rotting or putrefaction when the substance has been reduced to first matter. Then, having gone through many colors, the white stage is reached, and finally, at the end of the process the substance turns red. Several commentaries were published on these verses. Some 200 years after they were written, they were reprinted with a particularly detailed interpretation by someone calling himself Eiranaeus Philalethes. His true identity is not certain. Like so many alchemists, he is a shadowy figure, but he is thought to have been an *adept*—that is, an alchemist who has attained the secret of the Philosopher's Stone. He is also supposed to have been the only person to have successfully performed a transmutation in North America.

In Philalethes' interpretation of Ripley's poem, the toad represents gold. Its black and stinking decay stands for the stage of putrefaction, necessary to attain first matter. The juice of grapes that the toad drinks is philosopher's mercury, a strange substance, perhaps only understood by alchemists. The "secret den" to which the bloated toad retreats is really the hermetically sealed, egg-shaped glass vessel in which the various stages of the alchemical process take place. In his own strange language Philalethes described the amount of time needed for the various essential color changes to occur: "In six and forty or fifty days expect the beginning of intire Blackness; and after six and fifty days more, or sixty, expect the Peacocks Tayl, and Colors of the Rainbow; and after two and twenty days more, or four and twenty, expect *Luna* perfect, the Whitest White, which will grow more and more glorious for the space of twenty days, or two and twenty at the most: After which, in a little more increased Fire, expect the Rule of *Venus* for the space of forty days more; and after him the Rule of *Sol flavus* forty days, or two and forty: And then in a moment comes the Tyrian Color, the sparkling Red, the fiery Vermilion, and Red Poppy of the Rock . . ."

For all its deliberately obscure symbolism, this is obviously a report on the observation of a real experiment, and it is not difficult to compare it with the process described by J.K. At the same time, the magic nature of the process, the attempt to imitate nature, is also apparent. The total time required adds up to the nine months that is the period of human gestation, and each stage takes place under the influence of an appropriate planet according to the principles expressed by Agrippa. As for the symbols, they also contributed an extra dimension to the meaning of the writing: they were influenced by medieval philosophy which believed that things which were superficially alike possessed some underlying similarity of nature. Therefore the lion, which was proud and tawny-colored and walked in the Sun, was not only a suitable symbol for gold, but could be thought to be an actual aspect of the nature of gold. With animals and mythic beasts, with incidents from the legends of antiquity, with acrostics and anagrams, secret alphabets and ciphers, these early alchemists gradually wove a net of mystification which in the end even they themselves could not penetrate.

Right: woodcuts from one of the early printed works on alchemy, *The New Pearl of Great Price* by Petrus Bonus. It was printed by the Aldine press, Venice, in 1546. One scholar remarks that the rare existing copies almost always are in a dilapidated condition because they were so subject to accidents near the furnaces of the adepts, among whom the book was a great favorite. In this sequence of illustrations a crowned king (symbolizing gold) is petitioned by his son (mercury) and five servants (silver, copper, iron, tin, and lead) for some of his power. He says nothing, and is slain by mercury. After a series of dramatic happenings, each of which represents an alchemical operation, the king is restored to life, and finally is able to crown his son and servants, although one—possibly lead, which was viewed with some suspicion by alchemists—is missing in the last scene of the resurrected king.

1

2

3

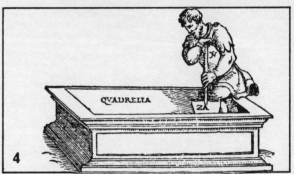

4

5

6

7

8

9

10

2. The alchemist and his *soror mystica*—the woman who is essential to the Work according to some alchemical theory—pray below the waters of the sky. Above them, angels support a vessel that holds Neptune with Sol and Luna, personifications of the sun and moon. Above the angels is the sun. The illustration apparently shows the answer to the alchemist's prayer, the divine revelation they have been waiting for. The vessel that the angels bring is a symbolic alembic for beginning the process.

3. Preparation for the work is shown in another introductory plate. The figure at the top with an eagle and a thunderbolt is probably Zeus. Beneath him is the created world, depicted in three concentric circles. The outer circle shows the air on top and the sea below. In the middle circle the earth is on top, and at the bottom the alchemist is fishing for Melusina. In the inner circle, the *soror* is fishing for Neptune, ruling beneath the waves.

The Wordless Book

The Wordless Book
The Wordless Book is unique among the old alchemical works. As its name implies, it is not written in words at all. Instead, its 15 engraved plates contain symbols only—and, unlike most other alchemical texts, it gives the full alchemical process from the start to the end.

1. Jacob lies sleeping at the foot of a ladder from earth to heaven, seeming to imply that heaven can be reached—or the Great Work achieved. The inscription is in Latin, and translated means: "The Wordless Book, in which nevertheless the whole of Hermetic Philosophy is set forth in hieroglyphic figures, sacred to God the merciful, thrice best and greatest, and dedicated to the sons of art only, the name of the author being Altus." The pseudonym "Altus" can be identified with the "Elder" or "Senior" of other alchemical literature, or possibly it refers to the Elder who plays a large part in the sequence of engravings in the book. One possible author is the French alchemist Jacques Tollé (1630-1696) who had a reputation as a transmuter. His Christian name of Jacques is French for "Jacob." The stone that the biblical Jacob used as a pillow, and upon which he poured oil, was an accepted symbol for the Philosopher's Stone.

4. The beginning of the Great Work. The *materia prima* gathered from cloths wrung out after having been exposed in the fields to sun and rain. Some authorities interpret this as meaning that May dew is essential; others that the *materia prima* is simply natural substances, despised because they are ordinary, but which the alchemist by his art can transmute into the Stone. The cow and bull in the field symbolize the male and female principles, used to indicate opposites in traditional alchemical theory.

5. The product gathered is distilled. In the first picture the matter is poured into the still over a furnace, and in the second picture the distillation is taking place, with the distillate being collected in a large vessel. Next the residue is ladled into a smaller vessel, which is given to a figure of ambiguous sexuality marked with the sign of Luna and carrying an infant, possibly representing the new moon. The distillate is then heated in a furnace which is marked "40." This may mean that the process is to be carried on for a period of 40 days.

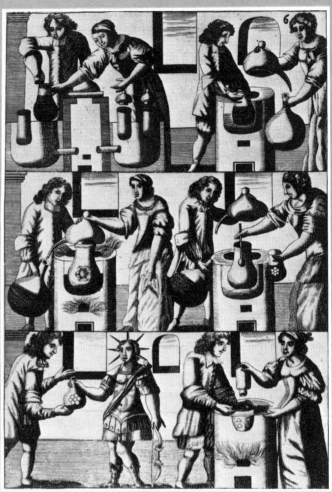

6. Further alchemical operations. First the distillate is poured into another container and subjected to further distillation. At this point the Golden Flower appears, possibly indicating the appearance of a crucial color. The residue liquid with the Golden Flower is ladled into a smaller vessel. The next illustration is ambiguous: is the liquid being offered to the sun gold Sol or being brought by him to the alchemist? In any case, the matter which has been calcinated into dust by the furnace is poured by the *soror* into yet another vessel over the fire.

9. The distillate is then exposed to nature, in the same way as the *materia prima* was originally gathered, with the dishes laid out as the cloths were. The rays coming down from heaven symbolize divine power. Then at the bottom, the calcinated matter is poured into a vessel. Mercury, with his staff and wings, is shown coming to give his assistance to the *soror* holding the flask.

7. Calcination and combination. In the first picture, the black ash is titurated, or turned into powder, and poured into an open dish. It is then transferred to an alembic, and when placed over the fire, has a liquid added to it. It is then stirred and ladled into a flask with four stars. The bottom pictures are the most difficult: a naked man (Saturn or Kronos?) sits on a bonfire, devouring his child, then sits—still with the infant—in a tub, while one distillate is poured over him, and later the infant is held by another naked man (the alchemist?) and a woman with the sign of Luna (the *soror*?) holds the flask with four stars. As Saturn was often a symbol for lead, perhaps lead is being transmuted by "infant's blood," an expression for the "mineral spirit of metals," using processes of calcination and ablution.

8. A new stage of the Work. The angels bring Mercury to improve the mixture. The birds flying upward represent matter released by calcination. At the bottom of the picture the alchemist and the *soror* pray and watch over the furnace while the new mixture brews in the alembic.

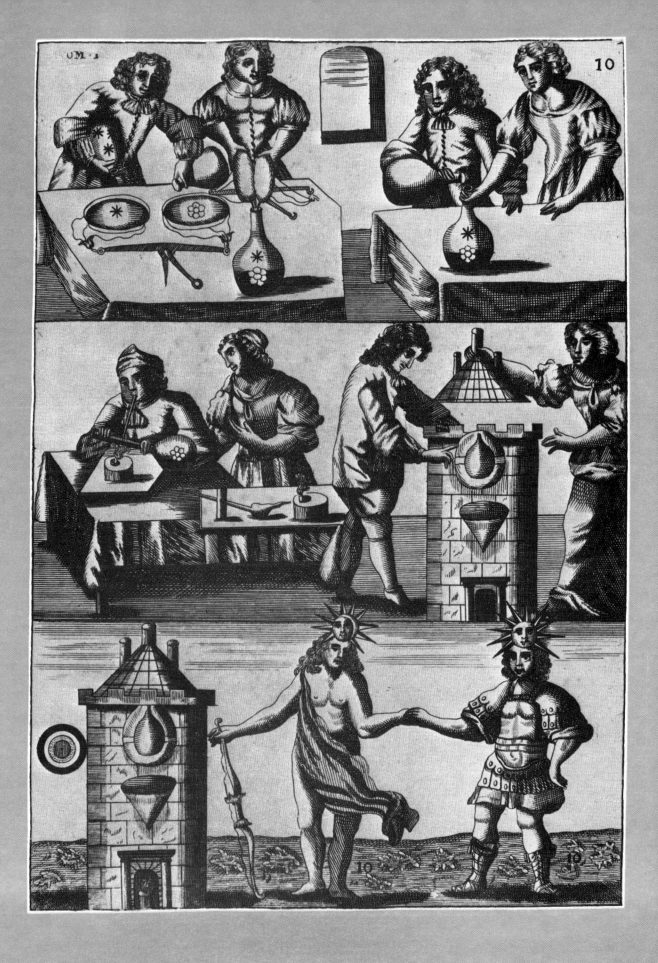

10. Equal weights of two substances, one marked with a star and the other with a flower, are combined and sealed in the Philosopher's Egg. The alchemist makes the fire by the most primitive method—presumably the most "natural" way—with a bow drill. The vessel is then placed in the athanor. Sol and Luna link hands to symbolize the amalgamation of the materials, presumably sophic mercury and sophic sulfur. The number 10 appears at the feet of each figure, and there is a target beside the athanor.

11. Mercury is again carried by angels in the alembic beneath the sun, while the alchemist and the *soror* pray by the side of their furnace. Curiously, alchemists believed that even with a process that would lead to success it was necessary for the substances to be subjected to the process over and over again. Repetition was a vital part of normal alchemical practice.

12. As in the ninth engraving, the distillate is taken back out again to nature, and Mercury's assistance is once again required. The repetition was considered to be absolutely crucial to the success of the Great Work.

15. In this final engraving the setting is the same as that of the first. An aged man—Jacob grown old or perhaps Mercurius—is crowned by cupids and helps the alchemist and *soror* to rise, leaving the body and animal nature as dead. They have no further need of the material ladder for their ascent. The scrolls read, "You depart seeing."

13. Again the substances are weighed, but an important change has taken place: the symbol of the flower has been replaced by the symbol of the sun. Again the fire is laboriously made, the Philosopher's Egg placed within the furnace, and Sol and Luna unite, but this time the numbers around their feet show multiplication—apparently the Stone that was activated in plate 10 now increases.

14. The ovens stand on the top row. Then the vessel is opened and the material weighed. Symbolic suns are on the stills at either side. At the bottom the alchemist and the *soror* are shown with the Philosopher's Egg between them. They vow secrecy—and the Great Work is completed.

The Wandering Alchemists

Of all the monarchs of Europe who dabbled in alchemy, the Emperor Rudolf II was by far the most enthusiastic. His laboratory in Prague, in the country then called Bohemia, occupied two rooms of an old one-story building having three great furnaces and their flues along one wall. One furnace was designed to produce great heat for the smelting of ores, the second heated a large *bain-marie* or water bath, and the third was kept at low heat for the distillation of volatile liquids. On this third furnace stood a huge cucurbit surmounted by five *helms* (caps or covers) one above the other, with their long necks fitting into phials to collect

During the 16th and early 17th centuries there were many enigmatic men who described themselves as alchemists and wandered from city to city, teaching the arts of transmutation to others, and then vanishing into obscurity again. Above: a medal that was struck from alchemical gold transmuted before His Highness Charles Philip, Count Palatine of the Rhineland on December 31, 1716. Right: a 16th-century miniature of an alchemist approaching a lady, probably representing an earth spirit, who gives life to plants and has a kind of darker magic. Thus the alchemist draws on the powers of earth for his work, indicated by the furnace.

81

"Kelley's story was plausible"

the distillates. The shelves along the other walls were crammed with alembics, descensories, pelicans, aludels and other pieces of apparatus, and there were glass jars, bottles, and gallipots, or glazed earthenware pots, packed with solids and liquids. A great wooden block in the center of one room held a vast mortar, with its pestle suspended from a rocking beam hanging from the rafters. On a ledge near one of the smoke-grimed windows lay well-thumbed books and old manuscripts, and a nearby table was piled with glass phials, pewter funnels, hourglasses of different sizes, spoons, spatulas, and knives. In the corridor between the two rooms were stocks of charcoal, nests of crucibles, clay and other materials for sealing the necks of flasks, and all kinds of pots and pans.

The alchemists who were encouraged to work in this laboratory lived nearby in a narrow street that wound steeply upward from the cloisters of Saint George's church toward Saint Vitus' cathedral. To this day it is known as Golden Lane. Close by lived Dr. Thaddeus Hajek, the court physician and director of the laboratory. On September 3, 1584, he received two visitors from England: Dr. John Dee and his assistant Edward Kelley.

Exactly what Dee was doing in Bohemia has been the subject of speculation for the past 400 years. He was a famous scientist, England's leading mathematician and navigational expert, the owner of the largest library in the land, court astrologer to Queen Elizabeth I, and almost certainly an important spy for his country. The previous September he had left England secretly with Kelley, their two wives, and a certain Polish count named Albert Laski, who had hopes of becoming the king of Poland. They had spent an unhappy winter in Cracow, Poland, and when Laski had run short of funds without seeing any improvement in his hopes of gaining the throne, he had suggested that the two Englishmen present themselves to the Emperor Rudolf II. Perhaps he thought they would be able to raise more money by demonstrating their skills at alchemy, because Kelley claimed to possess the Philosopher's Stone.

Kelley's story was plausible. According to him he was born Edward Talbot in Worcester in 1555, and he later studied for a time at Oxford without taking a degree. His father may have been an apothecary, which would account for the skill he possessed in chemistry, and he appears to have set himself up as a notary—that is, someone who witnessed legal documents. He was found to have forged some title deeds for one of his clients, and it is said that his ears were clipped for the offense. Certainly he always wore a close-fitting skull cap that concealed the tops of his ears. After his sentence he could no longer practice, and for some time he led a wandering existence in Wales. It was at this time that he seems to have changed his name to Kelley.

Staying in an inn outside Bristol one night, Kelley was shown an old manuscript by the innkeeper. This manuscript, it appeared, had been stolen from a monastery some years before, and it was said that it had been taken from the broken tomb of Saint Dunstan, the Abbot of Glastonbury. Kelley had some knowledge of Welsh and could make some sense of the old Celtic language. Moreover his experience as a notary had given him skill in deciphering old documents. He soon discovered that

Left: Emperor Rudolf II, who died in 1612. He was greatly interested in all aspects of the science of his time, being a patron of the astronomers Tycho Brahe and Johannes Kepler, but alchemy came to obsess his mind and near the end of his life he neglected the affairs of state. Haughty and suspicious, he was not popular. Below: the Golden Lane in Prague, which was also called the Street of the Alchemists, after the many men who worked for Rudolf II.

**Above: Edward Kelley, in a print
made about 1600, a few years
after his death. Medium, alchemist,
and convicted criminal, his role
in both magical and alchemical
transactions with John Dee has
always been disputed. Certainly
Dee believed Kelley was absolutely
essential to his work, and would
go to great lengths to please him.**

the manuscript was a treatise on alchemy. He concealed his
excitement, and asked the innkeeper whether anything else had
been taken from the tomb. Only two small ivory bottles that
had contained a red and a white powder, said the publican. He
had given them to his children as playthings, but he thought the
one containing the red powder was still intact. For the sum of
one guinea, Kelley could keep the manuscript and the bottle.

Early in 1582 Kelley turned up at Dr. John Dee's house just
outside London. At that time Dee had just begun his experiments in scrying or crystal-gazing. He had a glass sphere, and a
disk of polished black obsidian that had been brought from
Mexico by one of the early American explorers—both of which
are now in the British Museum. He called these two objects his
"shewstones," but he himself did not have the gift of "sight"
and he had to employ a medium to see and describe the visions
that appeared in them. Kelley proved to be a skillful scryer, and
soon he and Dee were spending every available moment in
conjuring up visions of spirits and angels. We do not know
whether he attempted to use his red powder at that time,
although some 80 years later Elias Ashmole, a well-known
archeologist and antiquarian, wrote that "Mr. Lilly [the
famous 17th-century astrologer] told me that John Evans in-
formed him that he was acquainted with Kelley's sister in
Worcester, that she showed him some of the gold her brother
had transmuted . . ."

There is no doubt, however, that Dee took his shewstones to
Cracow and to Prague, and that Kelley took his powder. When
they visited Dr. Hajek, the director of Emperor Rudolf's
laboratory in Prague, Kelley demonstrated a transmutation in
Hajek's cellar. Hajek then arranged an audience with the
Emperor, during which Kelley scryed with the shewstone. He
revealed through the medium of the spirit Zadkiel a formula for
the Philosopher's Stone, which the Emperor carefully copied
down. When Dee sought a second audience, he was told that the
Emperor was away hunting, and that he should make all his
communications in future through Dr. Kurtz, a member of the
council.

Dee and Kelley were very short of money by then: they had
been a year out of England, and Mrs. Dee had recently given
birth to a fourth child. Among Dee's papers in the British
Museum is a petition written for Jane Dee by Edward Kelley:

"We desire God, of his greate and infinite mercies to grant us
the helpe of His hevenly mynisters, that we may by them be
directed how or by whom to be ayded and released in this
necessitie for meate and drinke for us and for our familie,
wherewith we stand at this instant much opressed . . ."

Dee spent some time in trying to interest Dr. Kurtz in his experiments, and even turned down an offer of a salary of a
thousand marks from the Czar of Russia because he hoped for
more encouragement from the Emperor Rudolf. During his
time abroad Dee had been successfully spreading his own
religious and scientific beliefs. He was one of the foremost
thinkers of his age, and his ideas carried great weight. However,
they did not at all accord with those of the Catholic Church,
and in the spring of 1586 it became apparent that the Church

Above: a scene from *The Alchemist*, a play by Ben Jonson first presented in 1610. It features two charlatan alchemists, Subtle and Face—and it has been suggested that the prototypes for the characters were Dee and Kelley. The play's satiric barbs assume that the audience knows alchemical imagery and vocabulary well.

Above: one of the alchemical symbols from Edward Kelley's book *Theater of Terrestrial Alchemy*, showing the Philosopher's Egg. It was titled "Of the Exaltation of Mercurial Water" which was an essential element of his process.

was about to take action against both him and Kelley. They left Prague hurriedly, and learned not long after that it was just in time. The Pope's representative had accused them of conjuring and black magic, and had ordered Rudolf to arrest them and send them to Rome for interrogation.

For several months they wandered, until in September 1586 Count Wilhelm Rosenberg of Bohemia invited them to stay in his castle at Trebona. Kelley immersed himself in his alchemical experiments, and even Dee began to take a necessary interest in the subject. There are many stories that they succeeded in making gold: John Aubrey, the 17th-century writer and antiquarian, wrote that "Arthur Dee, his sonne, a physician at Norwich, and intimate friend of Sir Thomas Browne, told Mr.

Bathurst that (being but a boy) he was used to play at quoits with the plates of gold made by projection in the garret of Dr. Dee's lodgings. . . ." There is also a report in the manuscripts of Elias Ashmole that Queen Elizabeth was impressed by some of this gold. "On the continent Kelley annointed a warming pan belonging to a Mr. Willoughby with a certain oil which changed a portion of the lid to gold. This piece was cut out and, with the pan, sent to Elizabeth who, observing the perfect fit of the gold plate into the hole in the lid, was thus convinced of Kelley's powers."

The Emperor Rudolf, it seems, also became convinced of Kelley's powers. Kelley managed to make several visits to Prague without being arrested, and brought back large sums of money for Dee. He was even made "a Baron of the Kingdom of Bohemia," and insisted thereafter in calling himself Sir Edward Kelley. Poor Dee, with his shewstones, was pushed into the background, and in the autumn of 1589 he decided at last to return to England. But Kelley would not go with him. He was sure that, although his stock of red powder was almost exhausted, he could renew it by carefully following the instructions in one of his books. These included the *Book of Zacharias* with, as Dee had noted, "the Alkanor that I translated out of French . . . Rowlaschy his Third boke of Waters Philosophicall; the Boke called *Angellicum Opus*, all in pictures of the work

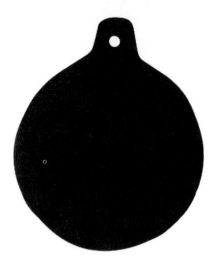

Left and below: one of John Dee's "shewstones," a black obsidian disk-shaped mirror, and the case for carrying it. Both shewstones (the other was a crystal globe) had to be suitably manipulated, and the spirits would then appear and deliver their messages to Kelley, who would dictate them to the waiting Dee.

The Failed Alchemist

If the golden rewards of success often dangled temptingly before alchemists and persuaded some of the weaker practitioners into fraud, the penalties for failure were often drastic. One who discovered this to his cost was Georg Honauer, who called himself Lord of Brunnhof and Grobschütz. He came to the court of Duke Frederick of Württemberg, who sought in the alchemist's art an answer to his own financial problems.

Honauer at first was successful, but to make sure of this, he had secretly thrown charcoal mixed with gold into the bubbling quicksilver in the crucible. Not content with this, he managed to satisfy another of the duke's tests by bringing a large chest with a secret compartment into his laboratory. After the duke had formally sealed up the room during the transmutation, the hidden accomplice emerged from the chest, and put the needed gold into the crucible.

Honauer was defeated when the duke presented him with iron weighing 52 hundredweight, and demanded that it be made into the finest gold. The duke had the iron covered with gold-leaf and made into gallows. On a fine spring day in 1597 he hanged his unsuccessful alchemist on the gleaming golden iron he had failed to transmute.

from the beginning to the end; the copy of the man of Budwise Conclusions for the Transmutation of Metalls and 40 leaves in 4°, entitled *Extractiones Dunstani*, which he himself extracted and noted out of Dunstan's his boke and the very boke of Dunstan was cast on the bed hard by the table."

Was this "very boke of Dunstan" the manuscript that Kelley had bought from the innkeeper? There are many who believe that it was, and that Kelley incorporated the teachings of this manuscript in his own book *The Stone of the Philosophers*. Dee's son Arthur, who later took the post in Russia that his father had refused, often referred to the *Book of Dunstan* in his writings.

Despite his extensive collection of reference material, Kelley appears to have had problems in duplicating the essential red powder. He continued his experiments, but both Count Rosenberg and the Emperor Rudolf became increasingly impatient. In England, impressed by the gold lid of the warming pan she had seen, Queen Elizabeth asked her Lord Treasurer to see whether he could persuade Kelley "to come over to his native countrie and honour her Majestie with the fruites of such knowledge as God has given him." Still Kelley would not come, and the Lord Treasurer finally wrote: "Many say that if you come not, it is because you cannot perform what has been reported of you. . . . I am expressly commanded by Her Majestie to require you to have regard to her honour . . . be assured of worldly reward, you can make your Queen so happie . . . surely as no subject she hath can do the like. Good Knight, let me end my letter, conjuring you in God's holy name not to keep God's gift from your natural countrie, but rather helpe make Her Majestie a glorious and victorious power against the mallyce of hers and God's enemies."

Then came news that Kelley was imprisoned by the Emperor on charges of sorcery and heresy. It was probably intended more as a warning than a punishment, because Kelley was allowed his books, and devoted the time to writing his treatise on the Philosopher's Stone. In 1593 he was once more at liberty, and even persuaded the Emperor to extend an invitation to Dee to revisit Prague—an invitation that Dee, then 66 and as always short of money, did not accept. In December of that year a certain Philip Gawdy wrote home: "Kelley is delivered out of prison and restored to his former estate and maketh gold as fast as a hen will cracke nuttes"—a most ambiguous remark when one considers the normal diet of the hen.

Shortly after this, Kelley was once more imprisoned, and his end remains a mystery. It was reported that he had twisted his bedclothes into a rope to escape from his prison, fell to the ground, broke both legs and a couple of ribs, and died some days later. There is some doubtful evidence that Dee had spoken to Elizabeth on his behalf, and that the escape had been engineered from England. Other reports stated that he had been killed in prison, and even that he had killed himself.

Dee, for the remaining 15 years of his life, gave up the practice of magic. Without Kelley as his link with the world of spirits he could only "dream after midnight of my working of the Philosopher's Stone with others." He died in December

1608 "firmly believing that the secrets of the Universe were still within his grasp and that, though he had proved unworthy to receive them in his lifetime, beyond the grave they would be vouchsafed to him."

Dee had many other reasons for his journey to Europe beside the desire to spread the knowledge of alchemy. But by the 17th century, many alchemists began to travel with that purpose chiefly in mind. Wandering emissaries appeared at various places on the continent. They would arrive unannounced in some town, make contact with the local alchemists, instruct them in the secrets of transmutation, and disappear again. The first of these was Alexander Seton, a Scot.

In 1601 Seton had given shelter to a Dutch sea captain, Jacob Haussen, whose ship had been driven ashore near Seton's house in Scotland. The following year, Seton turned up at Haussen's home in Enkhuisen, and confided to him that he was an adept. He said he had a mission to teach the art of transmutation. Before he left, he prepared for the skeptical sailor a bar of gold, and cut a time and date into it with a steel point. It was 4 p.m. on the afternoon of March 13, 1602.

From Enkhuisen Seton traveled to Amsterdam and Rotterdam, giving demonstrations of his skill in both cities. He took a ship from Rotterdam, disappearing for over a year. We next pick up his trail in Zurich, Switzerland, where he obtained a letter of introduction to the scientist Dr. Jacob Zwinger of Basel. He traveled to Basel in the company of Professor Wolfgang Dienheim of Freiburg, who wrote a detailed record of everything that took place. Part of this report follows:

"I . . . found myself traveling in company with a gentleman of remarkable intellectual gifts. He was short of stature and rather stout, with a high color, and sanguine temperament, and wore his brown beard trimmed in the French style. He was dressed in a suit of black satin, and was accompanied by one servant only, who was distinguishable from everyone else by his red hair and beard." Throughout the journey the two men disputed about alchemy and the possibility of transmutation, and in Basel they persuaded Dr. Zwinger to provide some slabs of lead, a crucible borrowed from a local goldsmith, and some ordinary sulfur.

"Setonius did not touch any of these things. He asked for a fire to be lit, ordered the lead and sulfur to be put in the crucible over the fire, the mass to be stirred, and the lid to be put on . . . At the end of a quarter of an hour he said: 'Throw this paper into the molten lead, but make sure that it goes right into the middle, and that none falls into the fire.' In the paper was a heavy sort of lemon-yellow powder—but you needed good eyesight to see it. Although we were as doubting as Saint Thomas himself, we did everything he told us. After the mass had been heated for another quarter of an hour and stirred continuously with little iron rods, the goldsmith was told to extinguish the fire by pouring water over it. We found not a vestige of lead remaining, only the finest gold which, in the opinion of the goldsmith, was of a quality better even than the excellent Hungarian or Arabian gold. It weighed exactly the same as the lead we had put in originally."

Zwinger confirmed this account in a letter to another professor in Basel, Emmanuel König, who later published it. The second letter also states that Seton performed a further transmutation before he left the city.

Seton seems next to have appeared in Strasbourg under the alias of Hirschberger. In that city he performed a transmutation in the shop of the goldsmith Gustenhöfer, and presented him with a small sample of his red powder before leaving. However, his visit eventually brought misfortune to the goldsmith. The Emperor Rudolf heard of his success, but only after he had used up the supply of powder. The Emperor summoned him to Prague and insisted that he perform a transmutation. The unfortunate Gustenhöfer confessed that the powder had been given him by a stranger, and he had no idea how to make any more. The Emperor refused to believe him and had him imprisoned for life.

Meanwhile Seton had traveled on to Frankfurt, where he

Above: Emperor Rudolf II in the laboratory of his alchemist, after a painting by Vaczlar Brozik. In fact he had many alchemists, and often visited them to watch their operations. Their failures were on occasion tolerated, but at other times punished by torture or death.

Right: Rudolf as the Roman god Vertumnus, an extraordinary portrait by Giuseppe Arcimboldo. Vertumnus was the god of changing seasons, and hence of flower and fruit. Rudolf, who was apparently eccentric to the point of madness, was immensely pleased by this portrait and ennobled the artist.

represented himself as a French count. He made friends with a merchant named Koch, who later wrote to the historian Theobald de Hogelande: "He did not put a hand to the work himself, but allowed me to do everything. He gave me a reddish-gray powder, weighing about three grains. I dropped it into two half-ounces of quicksilver in a crucible. Then I filled the crucible about halfway up with potash, and we put it over a gentle heat. After this I filled the furnace with charcoal, so that the crucible was entirely embedded in a very hot fire; I left it there for about half an hour. When the crucible was red hot, he told me to throw a little piece of yellow wax into it. A few minutes later, I cooled the crucible and broke it open. At the bottom I found a small piece of gold that weighed 54 ounces three grains. It was melted in my presence and submitted to an assay; 23 carats 15 grains of gold resulted, together with six of silver—both of an exceptionally brilliant color. I had a stud made for my shirt with part of the gold."

Seton next went to Cologne, where he demonstrated the art before the skeptical city surgeon Meister Georg and completely convinced him. He then traveled on to Hamburg. News of his exploits had spread all over the Rhineland, but because he constantly changed his alias, and because he went from city to city, he was nicknamed the Cosmopolite from the Greek meaning a citizen of the world. His destination after Hamburg was Munich, where he fell in love with a pretty girl and eloped with her. In the autumn of 1603 he reached Crossen, and Christian II of Saxony invited him to come to his court and demonstrate a transmutation.

Seton was deeply in love with his new wife and, rather foolishly, sent his servant Hamilton to court in his place. Hamilton successfully carried out a transmutation but, probably realizing the intentions of the Saxony ruler, hastily disappeared. Christian's greed, coupled with his feeling that he had been insulted by Seton's indifference and his fear that Seton would run away, caused him to make an immediate arrest of Seton.

Christian II wanted no less than full details of how to prepare the red powder for himself, but Seton had sworn never to reveal the secret. He was thrown into prison and tortured over and over again, but nothing would persuade him to tell the ruler what he wanted to know.

At this point in the story a certain Michael Sendivogius, who lived near Cracow, appeared on the scene. He heard of Seton's imprisonment and decided, with ulterior motives, to help him escape. He sold his house in Cracow and used the money to ingratiate himself with Seton's jailers. One night, having got them drunk, he unlocked the prisoner's cell and carried out the weak and broken man. Stopping only to pick up Seton's wife and her supply of the Philosopher's Stone, he drove his carriage at breakneck speed through the night until the party was safely out of Saxony.

But, even out of gratitude for his rescue, Seton would not reveal his secret. Shortly afterward he died from the effects of his terrible tortures. Sendivogius married Seton's widow, and inherited the supply of red powder; but although he spent years experimenting he could find no way to make more. He went to

Above: Christian II of Saxony, before whom Alexander Seton made a successful transmutation. The Elector was determined to discover his secret, and when Seton refused to tell him, had him tortured.

Right: an alchemist being tortured by an avaricious ruler. Christian II, who had Seton put through similar ordeals, found himself at length in an unfortunate dilemma. Seton, still stubborn about not revealing how he produced red powder, was clearly near to death, and if he died the secret would be lost forever. Christian then reluctantly gave up on his attempt to extract the information and put him in solitary confinement. Sendivogius, who was a stranger to Seton, rescued him from jail—mainly in the hope of discovering the gold-making secret himself.

Above: Michael Sendivogius in a stylized portrait published in 1624. His early career is obscure. It has been reported that he was the natural son of a Polish nobleman, but certainly he had no success in alchemy until he encountered Alexander Seton.

Prague and showed the Emperor Rudolf how to carry out a transmutation. The Emperor had a marble plaque carved, which may be seen to this day, with the Latin words *Faciat hoc quispiam alius quod fecit Sendivogius Polonus*—"Whoever else could do what Sendivogius the Pole has done?"

On his way back from Prague to Cracow, Sendivogius was taken prisoner by a nobleman who hoped to have more success with him than Christian II had had with Seton. Sendivogius kept a little of his wonderful powder in a gold box, which he hung around his neck, but most of it was hidden in a hole cut in the step of his carriage, and the nobleman did not find it. The prisoner managed to get hold of a file and cut through one of the bars of his cell window. Then, tying his clothes into a rope, he escaped naked into the night and fled back to Prague. There he told his story to the Emperor, who confiscated the nobleman's estate and presented it to Sendivogius.

But the red powder did not last forever, and soon Sendivogius had spent everything he had in trying to manufacture more. In the end he was reduced to borrowing money from various acquaintances, and borrowing more when he was forced to repay his first loans. He earned a little by writing alchemical treatises, for which he took the name of the Cosmopolite to give them greater authority. He died, a near pauper, in 1646.

There were other wandering adepts, all of whom were vouched for by distinguished scholars, and dozens of learned books published throughout Europe in the first half of the 17th century with detailed descriptions of transmutations. But alchemy's flourishing days were numbered. The scientific revolution had begun.

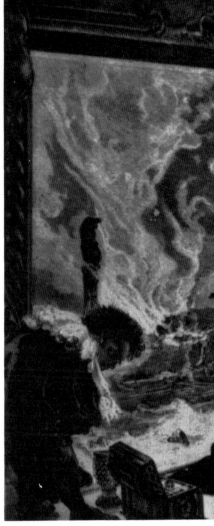

Above: Sendivogius making gold —presumably using Seton's red powder because he failed once it was used up— in the royal castle in Cracow before King Sigismund III and a Jesuit priest. The fireplace shown here was still to be seen in the castle as late as 1950.

Right: a piece of alchemical gold now in the British Museum, shown here magnified about four times. The accompanying label—in 19th-century handwriting—states that it was made in Bapora in October 1814, in the presence of Colonel Macdonald and Doctor Colquhoun.

6

What Happened to Alchemy?

Since its beginnings in the early centuries after Christ, Western alchemy had been a strange tightly woven network of varied beliefs and practices. No two ideas were more closely linked than the belief that the quest to transmute ordinary metals into gold went hand in hand with a quest for spiritual perfection. For the true alchemist, the struggles in the laboratory reflected the struggles in his soul. As he seemed to approach nearer his physical aim of making gold, so he came nearer to his spiritual aim of a perfect soul. This explains the fact that in true alchemy, the desire for gold had nothing whatever to do with the desire for riches. Indeed,

As the 17th century progessed, time and enlightenment in other fields caught up with alchemy. The idea of hidden mysteries was changed by the concept of repeatable experiments and an open exchange of scientific views between experimenters. The scientific method was born, and alchemists found themselves having to cope with the consequences. Right: in this painting of *The Discovery of Phosphorus*, the dazzled alchemist kneels awestruck before the luminous spectacle of phosphorus within his receiver.

97

"Early alchemists... discovered many new substances and methods of treatment"

alchemists were not interested in amassing fortunes. The ability to make gold was a sign that they had reached a state of inward perfection and discovered the secret workings of the Universe. Of course there were always alchemists who became so involved in the spiritual quest that they neglected the practical aims of the laboratory, and those who became so absorbed in the practical side that they neglected their spiritual development. But ideally, until the decline of alchemy, the practical search for the perfect metal and the spiritual search for the perfect soul were inseparable.

Like almost every Western scientist and philosopher up to the 17th century, alchemists unquestioningly accepted Aristotle's theory of the Universe. According to him, all material things in the world were composed of varying proportions of the four elements of Earth, Air, Fire, and Water. But substances could be altered into other substances by the appropriate application of one of the four qualities of wetness, dryness, cold, or heat. This idea of change was fundamental to the alchemist's belief that base metals could be transmuted into gold.

Another important contribution to alchemy was made by the mystical and hermetic beliefs that arose in the early years of the Christian era, and were revived, with the ideas of Aristotle, in the Middle Ages and early Renaissance. Man, the Microcosm, was thought to be a reflection on a small scale of the Universe or Macrocosm. All things in the Universe were linked in harmony with each other. Man could discover and use this harmony for his own benefit, primarily through the system of correspondences that outlined a special relationship between certain planets, feelings, and objects, and ultimately by discovering the universal spirit that permeated the Universe. It was this spirit that the alchemists were attempting to identify and possess in the Philosopher's Stone.

When alchemy first developed in the early centuries after Christ, it was able to draw on the technical achievements of the Ancient World. In the previous 3000 years many crafts had become highly developed, and a vast amount of knowledge and expertise had been accumulated in many fields. Craftsmen had become expert in metalwork and glassmaking. The preparation of dyes, perfumes, and cosmetics, not to mention drugs and poisons, was highly skilled and had led to a detailed knowledge of many chemical compounds. In Egypt, one of the earliest and most influential civilizations, craftsmen produced the most beautiful objects for the rich in gold, silver, and precious stones. With equal skill, and for their poorer customers, they produced excellent imitations in colored alloys that could pass for gold, and colored glass that looked deceptively like real gems.

The early alchemists therefore had at their disposal a great deal of useful information about substances, highly skilled techniques, and the basic equipment. However, they were also innovators. They adapted and invented apparatus in order to carry out the endless processes of heating and cooling, separating and combining, vaporizing and solidifying that they deemed so essential to their task. In their ceaseless search for the Philosopher's Stone, they discovered many new substances and methods of treatment. By the 16th century the alchemist's

Above: opening of a course of
Lectures in Transmutative Chemistry, from a book by Annibal
Barlet. With such lectures given
in public—a world away from the
secretive private instruction
expressed in illusions and wary
symbolism—some alchemists moved
toward the science of chemistry.

Right: Francis Bacon, Viscount
St. Albans, after the marble tomb
effigy in the church in St. Albans.
He once wrote that alchemists were
like the sons of the man who told
them he had left gold buried in
the vineyard. By their vigorous
digging they found no gold, but
by turning up the mold around
the roots of the vines, produced a
a plentiful vintage. So, said
Bacon, did the attempts to make
gold bring to light many useful
inventions and instructive experiments for others to make use of.

Above: a meeting of the Royal Society, the national academy of science for Great Britain and Northern Ireland. The Society began about 1645 as a weekly gathering of a group of thinkers who had been influenced by "the New or Experimental Philosophy" that Francis Bacon advocated.

Left: King Charles II, who gave the Royal Society its first charter in 1660, and so helped chemistry establish itself as a nonmystical field of study.

laboratory was an extremely sophisticated place, in many ways resembling a modern chemical laboratory. But the alchemist was far from being a chemist in our sense of the term.

Chemistry, as we know it today, deals with the structure, composition, and properties of substances, and the way they react under different conditions. Before coming to any general conclusion, a chemist will repeat an experiment many times under identical conditions, and will keep careful records of the results. The alchemist's only interest in substances until the 16th century was as the possible ingredients of the Philosopher's Stone. Alchemists were not concerned to examine them further because they had a ready-made answer as to the nature of substances—first in the theory of the four elements of Aristotle, and

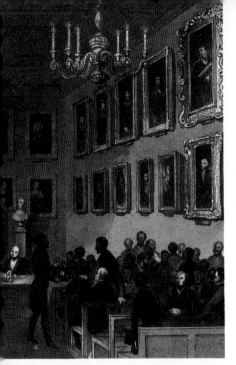

Above: Robert Boyle. Although he did his utmost to establish chemistry as an independent branch of natural philosophy, separate from both the gold-seeking alchemists and the medically minded followers of Paracelsus, he did believe in the possibility of transmutation.

then in the additional division of substances into sulfur and mercury or sulfur, mercury, and salt of later alchemists. Their belief in a mystical, hermetic philosophy, with its ideas of occult sympathies between objects, encouraged them to wild flights of fancy and speculation, often on the basis of a single observation. Many single chemical facts were established by the alchemists, but each existed in isolation and was of little general use.

It was Paracelsus, the great 16th-century physician, who perhaps unwittingly started the decline in alchemy and the progress toward true chemistry. A more than life-size figure himself, he embraced the mystical and the practical aspects of alchemy in revolutionary ways. Brushing aside the question of transmuting metals to gold, he insisted that the true purpose of mystical alchemy was to develop secret powers within one's soul, and the true goal of practical alchemy was to find medical cures. His followers found both these ideas too much to contend with. Some retreated from the laboratory to concentrate on their spiritual development. Others, joyfully released from the rigidity of searching for the Philosopher's Stone, began to experiment more constructively. In so doing they made many important new discoveries. The foundations were laid first for *iatro*, or medical chemistry, and then for chemistry itself.

Gradually hermetic beliefs in the unity of the cosmos fell out of fashion, and scientists began to look for new theories to supplement or replace Aristotle's ideas. Many throughout the 17th and early 18th centuries continued to believe in the possibility of transmuting metals to gold, but they were too busy either with their own souls or with their laboratory experiments to look closely into the question. Creating gold from base metals fell into the hands of those who hoped to amass riches or to dupe others, which was a far cry from the spiritual aims of the early alchemists.

Scientific ideas from other sources also gradually began to erode the position of alchemy in the 16th and 17th centuries. Francis Bacon, the great English essayist and scientific philosopher who died in 1626, had insisted on the need for properly organizing experiments and recording results so that they could be repeated and verified. He believed that experiments should lead to generalizations, which in turn would lead to new experiments. These ideas were revolutionary to the alchemist, whose experiments were largely haphazard, rarely repeated, and certainly never led toward any scientific conclusion. Bacon also suggested that scientists from different fields should meet together to discuss their work and exchange ideas. Alchemists were used to working in secret, jealously guarding their ideas and only communicating by means of obscure and almost incomprehensible symbolism. The open discussions between groups of eminent scientists and thinkers that began to take place in Europe from the mid-16th century onward dealt yet another blow to the mysterious image of the alchemist.

In England in 1660 Charles II helped inaugurate just such a scientific group by founding the Royal Society of London. One of its first members, Robert Boyle, was instrumental in setting chemistry on its feet as a science in its own right, freeing it both

Right: Heinrich Khunrath at prayer in his laboratory. Khunrath, who died in 1605, was one of the alchemists who moved toward a deeply mystical approach to the art. His working place, as shown here, is half church and half laboratory, adorned with many inscriptions. Among them are these: "When we attend strictly to our work, God himself will help us" and "That which is wisely tried again will succeed sometime"— no doubt a comfort in moments of alchemical melancholia.

from the aims of transmuting metals and from preparing medicines. In the *Sceptical Chymist*, published in 1661, he attacked both the Aristotelian idea of four elements, and the alchemist's notion of the three principles of salt, sulfur, and mercury. He gave a totally new definition of an element as a substance that could not be broken down into component parts. Boyle was extremely interested in a new element that, according to tradition, had been discovered by a German alchemist named Brandt in the city of Hamburg. Boyle obtained a sample of this substance, which we know as phosphorus today, and with the help of an assistant, began to manufacture it. The product soon sold widely throughout Europe. Although Boyle's influence was strong, some scientists continued to

accept Aristotle's ideas until late in the 18th century. In the controversy, it is not surprising that many alchemists retreated from the scientific fray into the comparative safety of mysticism.

One of the strangest manifestations of alchemical mysticism is the story of the Rosicrucian fraternity, an order that claimed to possess immense power and to count as members the great alchemists of two centuries. All that is known of it is contained in three anonymous pamphlets published in Germany between 1614 and 1616. They are full of the strange symbolism that is so beloved of mystical alchemists, and are extremely difficult to understand. They gave no information on who the leaders of the fraternity were or where they were to be found. No one to this day has been able to determine whether the brother-

Above: the tomb of Christian Rosenkreuz, who is shown as the man at the bottom of the picture. The tomb synbolizes the Hill of the philosophers, covered with alchemical symbols. If the spiral path were followed, it would lead through all the processes to the crowning work at the top. By this time, mystical alchemy— of which Rosicrucianism is one of the most elaborate forms— had moved far beyond the original goal of transmuting metal to gold.

hood actually existed, whether it had been invented to convey certain ideas in symbolic terms, or whether it was a hoax designed to discredit eager dabblers in alchemy and the occult. The publication of the pamphlets aroused intense excitement and eager speculation in Europe. Many believers tried to get in touch with the authors, some by publishing their own pamphlets in reply. The interest lasted throughout the 17th century. Even famous scientists and philosophers such as Descartes and Leibniz tried hard to get at the truth, but without success.

The first of the pamphlets, *Fama Fraternitatis*, tells of the travels of Brother C.R.C. in search of scientific skills and true wisdom. C.R.C. was thought to stand for Christian Rosenkreuz, the last name meaning "Rosy Cross." Rosenkreuz settled in Germany and founded the Rosicrucian Order, or Fraternity of the Rosy Cross, with three other monks. They assisted him in writing down everything he had learned in science, magic, and healing. Gradually the order was increased to eight members. They later dispersed, having pledged to keep the identity of the fraternity secret for 100 years. Long after his death the tomb of Christian Rosenkreuz was said to have been opened, and his body found in a perfect state of preservation. The *Fama* aroused such excitement and interest that it had to be reprinted many times.

In 1615 the *Confessio* appeared. It was written in the same vague language, and though it invited readers to join the Brotherhood, it did not say how this could be done. The third pamphlet, *The Chemical Wedding*, was published in 1616. Even apart from its title, there was no doubt that *The Chemical Wedding* was inspired by alchemy. It was full of familiar alchemical symbols as well as much else that would appeal to the Renaissance magician, such as mathematical puzzles, descriptions of wonderful mechanical toys, and "most strange Figures, and dark Sentences and Speeches." In it, a Christian Rosenkreuz who may or may not be the same one as in the first pamphlet, is

invited to a royal wedding. After encountering various hazards, he reaches the castle, and there submits to certain tests. Finally he witnesses the marriage, and afterward is made a Knight.

Many years later a well-known German theologian, Johann Valentin Andreae of Würtemberg, confessed that he had written *The Chemical Wedding* as a schoolboy joke. Whether he was also the author of the other two pamphlets, and whether they were also intended as jokes, was unclear. However, even after this confession, many continued to take all the pamphlets seriously. At one level they were interpreted by occultists as describing various alchemical and hermetic secrets. Others read into them a deeper social purpose in which a reformation in science, similar to the Lutheran reformation in religion, was

Below: a 17th-century drawing of the ship of the argonauts, a float in the wedding pageant of Princess Elizabeth in 1613. In Greek myth the argonauts were a group of sailors who searched for the Golden Fleece—an obvious tie-in with the Chemical Wedding, in which another kind of search for gold goes on. The alliance of the Protestant German prince and the Protestant English princess was also seen as an immensely hopeful and important political event.

105

The Twelve Keys of Basil Valentine

This mysterious set of 12 illustrative emblems, each with its allegorical description or, as it was called, "explanation," had enormous popularity during the 17th century. Basil Valentine is probably a pseudonym for the author, a Rosicrucian mystical alchemist. No one knows what the author's true name was, or even when he might have lived. Above: The First Key, or the preparation of the materials of the Great Work. Gold (the king) is purified by antimony (the wolf); silver (the queen) is purified by cupellation with lead (the old man).

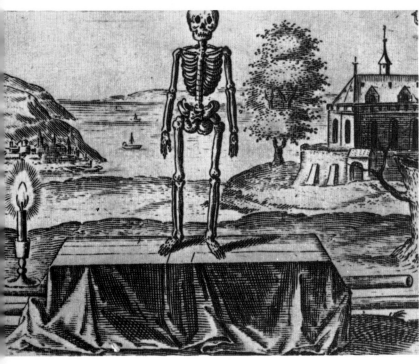

Above: The Second Key. The illustration shows Mercury, uniting the symbols of the sun and moon, or gold and silver. The commentary emphasizes the need for using only pure ingredients: "the king and his spouse must be quite naked when they are joined together."

Far left: The Third Key. As the commentary puts it: "then the cock will swallow the fox, and having been drowned in the water and quickened by the fire, will in its turn be swallowed by the fox." The process involves the preparation of "fiery sulfur."

Left: The Fourth Key. Here the common alchemical allegory of death followed by resurrection is used to represent steps in which the matter seems to disappear, and after some further alchemical processes is then found to have reappeared, purified.

Above: The Fifth Key. In ambiguous commentary Valentine writes: "Moreover, as iron as its magnet which draws it with the invisible bonds of love, so our gold has its magnet, vis., the first Matter of the great Stone. If you understand these my words, you are richer and more blessed than the whole world."

Right: The Sixth Key. The union of the king and queen, using the apparatus shown. The commentary emphasizes the necessity for getting proportions of substances used exactly right: "For this part of our Magistery skill is needed, in order to divide and compound the substances aright, so that the art may result in riches, and the balances may not be falsified by unequal weights."

Right: The Seventh Key. The four seasons are shown surrounding aqua, or water. The commentary is concerned with the degree of heat used in the processes, saying it should be as carefully attuned to the needs of the substances as the sun's heat during the seasons is to the needs of the earth.

Below: The Eighth Key. Again the theme of death and resurrection is used to explain that the material of the Great Work dies, or blackens, in the Philosopher's Egg, but later goes through a "revivifying" white stage. The two crossbowmen possibly indicate the difference between the adept and the puffer (one interested in gold-making only). The adept scores a direct hit, but the puffer's arrows fly at all angles.

Left: The Ninth Key. This is seen as showing lead falling from its place, to be replaced by Luna, or sophic mercury, but her feet are upon the phoenix, symbol of re-vivification, and of the Stone, which will change lead "until the glorious color of the triumphant king has been attained." The three serpents are the symbols for mercury, sulfur, and salt.

Below: The Eleventh Key. This is expressed as a parable, the story of a gilded knight, Orpheus, and his childless wife, Euridice. In a dream a winged messenger told Orpheus that he should take blood from his right side and the left side of his wife, and mix them together in "the globe of the seven wise Masters." From this mixture, made over and over again, will come children. Basil Valentine's comment adds, "I *may* not express myself more explicitly."

Right: The Tenth Key. The symbols of the sun, moon, and mercury are surrounded with emblems of holiness. The Latin motto across the top, the least ambiguous of those around the triangle, means "I am born of a male/female duality."

Below: The Twelfth Key. At this point it is assumed that the adept has managed to produce the Stone, and this Key is instruction on how to use it. The commentary says, "In dealing with this . . . I will drop my parabolic and figurative style, and plainly set forth all that is to be known." The Stone is to be combined with the best gold, refined with antimony, one part to three parts, and gently heated in a smelting pot for 12 hours, then melted for three further days and nights. The resulting tincture will then transmute metal, one part to 1000 parts, into "good and fixed gold."

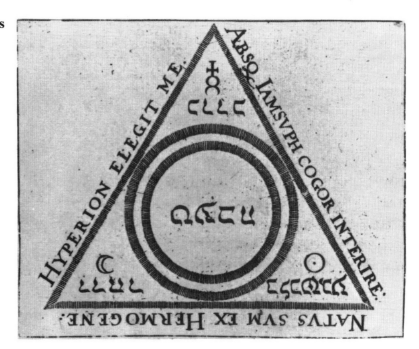

advocated. They argued that if greed and fraud were eliminated from science, and proper methods of research and experiment established, it would be of great benefit to humanity. Since it was not clear how anyone could join the Rosicrucians, some less scrupulous, or more excitable, people claimed that they were already members, or founded orders of their own.

One such person was Michael Maier, a successful physician who was born in Rendsberg, Germany in about 1568. He had been ennobled for his medical skill by the Emperor Rudolf II, but he seems to have become infected by that ruler's passion for alchemy. He abandoned medicine and devoted his later life to the pursuit of the Philosopher's Stone, losing both his health and his fortune in the process. When the Rosicrucian controversy broke he played a prominent role, defending the fraternity's claims in several tracts. He claimed both to be a member of the Rosicrucian Order, and to have founded a similar order himself. He visited the alchemical writer, Robert Fludd, in England, and converted him to Rosicrucian ideas. Fludd later published his own defense of Rosicrucianism.

Jacob Boehme was another supporter of the Rosicrucians. He was born in Germany in 1575 and started work as an itinerant shoemaker. When he finally settled down, he began to study alchemy. He soon abandoned the practical work, but he used the symbolic language of alchemy to describe his mystical visions. The Philosopher's Stone became the Spirit of Christ which must tincture the individual soul.

It was the mysterious nature of alchemical symbolism that enabled alchemists to make such differing interpretations. Some symbols could be interpreted as parts of the laboratory process, or as stages in the progress of the soul, or as both. Alchemy used an extraordinarily rich variety of symbolism, drawing on astrology, religion, and magic. Alchemists had always been concerned to preserve secrecy about their work, and symbols served a dual purpose. They were a convenient way of remembering things without writing them down, and they were an equally convenient way of confusing others when written down. There was no consistency in alchemical language, which often had hundreds of different symbolic terms for each of the various substances and processes. An outsider would be totally baffled by an alchemical manuscript, and even an experienced alchemist might spend years in trial and error attempting to decipher it. A few symbols were generally understood, but they rarely amounted to a set of instructions. The black crow, for example, represented the stage of putrefied matter, and the dove the pure white substance obtained by sublimation. The red king stood for gold, or philosopher's sulfur, and the white queen for silver, or philosopher's mercury. The toad stood for earthy matter, the winged lion was mercury, and the wingless lion was sulfur. The gray wolf stood for antimony, and the newborn baby with a crown for the Philosopher's Stone.

The 17th century was a time of great progress in both scientific thought and discovery, but strangely enough, many pioneering experimenters and philosophers were also staunch believers in alchemy. One of the most famous of these was Sir

Above: Michael Maier, 16th-century physician and Rosicrucian with a keen interest in alchemy. He assembled a collection of alchemical writings he called *The Golden Tripod*, which consisted of translations of three books, one of them being Valentine's *12 Keys*.

Right: illustration from a book by Robert Fludd, published in 1619, showing the functioning of the senses, the imagination, and the intellect in the mind. Fludd was an English Paracelsist physician, who was most impressed by the Rosicrucian pamphlets. He wrote two short books expressing his admiration for the Rosicrucians and ending with a plea that they should allow him to join them.

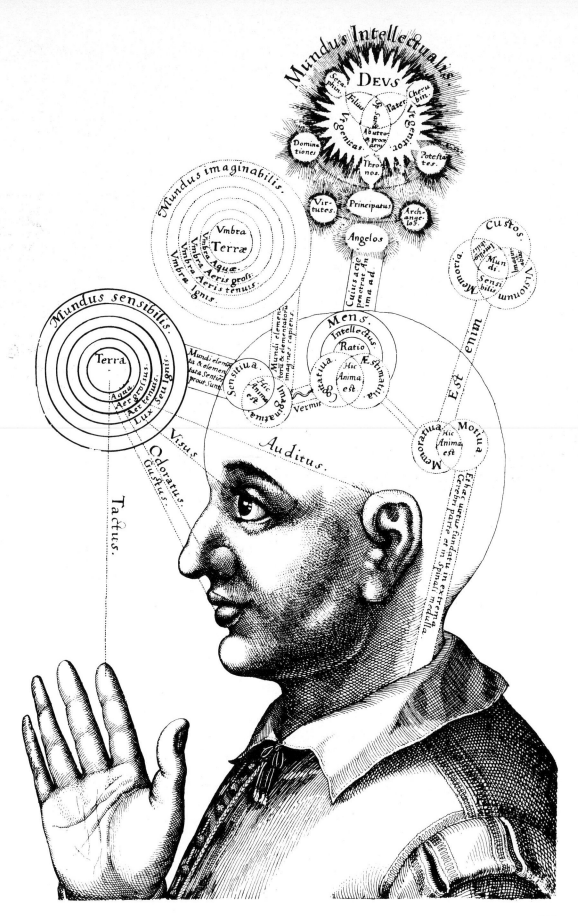

Above: Sir Isaac Newton, famed as the man who first stated the Law of Gravitation. In spite of his present-day reputation as a strictly scientific thinker, he was much interested in alchemy.

Isaac Newton, who propounded the law of gravity. He spent much time speculating on alchemy and the magical nature of things, and his mathematical investigations confirmed his belief in the mystical harmonies of the Universe. For example, although there were only six distinct colors in the spectrum, Newton felt obliged to identify seven because of the magical significance of this number. His description of gravity was at first viewed with great suspicion by fellow members of the Royal Society. Gravity, or *gravitas*, was a quality associated with the planet Saturn and the metal lead. The whole thing smacked too much of alchemy and magic. Only Newton's faultless mathematics preserved his reputation.

Newton was not the only important thinker to believe in alchemy. Descartes, who is regarded by many as being the father of modern philosophy, was deeply interested in the subject. Leibniz, another great philosopher, spent several formative years as secretary to an alchemical society in Nürnberg. He retained a life-long preoccupation with the nature of the Philosopher's Stone. A rather more eccentric figure was Johann Rudolf Glauber. Born in Germany in 1604, he became a physician and chemist, and was an ardent believer in alchemy. He made many important discoveries, especially in the chemistry of wines and the distillation of spirits. On examining the waters of a mineral spring where he had gone to take a cure, he found them to contain what we now know as sodium sulfate. Overjoyed, he believed that at last he had found one of the vital constituents of the Philosopher's Stone. Crystallized sodium is known as Glauber's Salt to this day. It is used not as an elixir of life, however, but as a laxative.

One important scientist who claimed to have carried out a successful transmutation was John Baptist van Helmont. He lived near Brussels and devoted his life to chemical investigation. He was the first man to identify gases as a distinct group of substances, and to distinguish between them in terms of their chemical and physical properties. His reputation for integrity was unquestioned. He was also a firm believer in alchemy. He tells how in 1618 he received a visit from a stranger who gave him a minute particle of the Philosopher's Stone, which he described as "of color such as saffron in its powder, yet weighty and shining like unto powdered glass." Van Helmont heated about eight ounces of mercury in a crucible and added the powder. "Straightway all the Quicksilver with a certain degree of noise stood still from flowing and being congealed settled like unto a yellow lump; but after poring it out, the bellows blowing, there were found eight ounces and a little less than eleven grains of gold." Van Helmont was convinced he had turned mercury into gold, and called his new son Mercurius in celebration of the event.

However, not all those interested in alchemy were sincere in their beliefs. As it began to decline, alchemy attracted many rogues and charlatans who saw it as a means to easy riches—though not through transmutation. By means of tricks such as hollow stirring rods, or crucibles with false bottoms, they were able to convince many gullible onlookers that they possessed

Above: J. B. van Helmont and his son F. M. van Helmont. Both he and his sons were doctors. The father claimed to have performed transmutations, using a saffron-colored powder that had been given him by a mysterious stranger.

LE MARQUIS DE FORCE-NATURE EN HABIT DE LABOURATOIRE.
Dr Dwangh angius Naturalis of gewaande Herschepper der Metaalen.

Herr Blasius Rauchmantl, der frucht-loszen ALCHIMIE Kunst
ARCHI-SECTATOR, QUINTÆ ESSENTIÆ STULTORUM POSSESSOR.
Ein Meister lasz ich mich der Elementen nennen,
Die ich Zusammen fug und wider kan zertrennen,
Kalt sie verarestirt im Kolben, schik sie auch

Left: a caricature called *Marquis of Outrage-Nature in his Laboratory Dress*, published in 1716. By then the public was more geared to the rationalist thought of Newton and the scientists, and found the trappings of the traditional alchemists comical.

115

Above: *Scientific Researches*, a caricature by Thomas Gilray, published in 1802. Not only were the alchemists the butt of jokes, but the chemists as well, with their paraphernalia and the remarkable results they claimed.

the secret of making gold. Borrowing money on the pretext of financing further transmutations, they would disappear before anyone had time to realize that he or she had been duped.

In one celebrated case in the 18th century the motive for deception appears to have been fame rather than money, but the trickster was cornered by investigators and the whole episode ended in tragedy. James Price was born as James Higginbotham in London in 1722. He studied at Oxford, took a series of degrees, and soon established a reputation as a chemist. In 1781, in accordance with the wishes of a relative who had left him a large sum of money, he changed his name to Price. In the same year he was elected to the Royal Society, and in 1782 he moved to a country house in the southeast of England. He soon announced to his astonished friends that he had succeeded in performing a transmutation in his private laboratory.

Various highly distinguished men were invited to his home to witness his experiments. First he added a small quantity of white powder to some mercury. This was mixed with a flux of borax and niter and then heated in a crucible. When the crucible had cooled it was found to contain an ingot of silver

equal in weight to the amount of mercury used. The same kind of procedure was followed again, this time using a red powder, and the crucible was found to contain an ingot of gold. The metals were tested and found to be genuine. They were exhibited to King George III, and caused an enormous sensation.

Price published a pamphlet describing these experiments which created great interest in the scientific world. In a second edition of the pamphlet he stated that his supply of the powders necessary for the transmutations was exhausted, and that the cost of preparing new powders in terms of time and his own health would be too great. However, the controversy aroused by his claims was so great that the Royal Society felt bound to investigate them officially. Unwillingly Price agreed to prepare new stocks of the powders. He was given six weeks to do so. On the appointed day the representatives arrived. Price showed them into his laboratory, excused himself for a moment, and on leaving the room, drank a concoction of prussic acid. He returned and died before their eyes. A verdict of death while of unsound mind was recorded. It was the last occasion on which a learned scientific association was prepared to officially investigate the claims of alchemy.

Above: Sir Joseph Banks. At the time that the Royal Society was investigating the alchemical claims of James Price, Sir Joseph was president of the Society.

7

Sex and Symbolism

In six centuries of manuscripts and books on the Western European alchemical tradition, there seems to be no obvious reference to sex. True, phrases such as "the chemical wedding" and "the faire Whyte Woman married to the Ruddy Man" keep recurring, but these are symbolic of stages in the alchemical process. Although for 600 years all kinds of accusations were leveled at "false Alchymists, who use all manner of filthy things," it was never suggested that alchemy involved anything of a sexual nature. The alchemical tradition was one of hard work and modest ascetism. It was only in the 18th and 19th centuries, when ideas from the

Although their symbolism and much of the imagery used sexual themes, the alchemists of the West used these references only to describe stages in the Great Work. For the alchemists of the East, however, for whom the transmutation of metals held no interest, sex played a very important role in their conception of the art itself.

Above: a 17th-century manuscript illustration, showing a copulating couple, to symbolize that within the putrefaction of the black stage generation is taking place. They pass through death to produce a perfect child, the elusive Stone.

Right: an Indian painting of about 1800. In eastern alchemy—as here, in Tantra—sexual intercourse became the method by which the adept moved toward the spiritual goal.

"Taoist alchemists... prime quest was the secret of immortality"

East began to reach Europe, that it became apparent that a different sort of alchemy had for a long time been practiced in China and India. This was a sexual alchemy. The transmutation took place entirely within the alchemist who sought through various sexual, respiratory, and mental practices to achieve immortality through union with the Universe.

The Chinese alchemists were usually followers of Taoism, one of the great religions of China. Its founding is traditionally ascribed to Lao-tzu in the 6th century B.C., although its roots probably go back much further. Lao-tzu is said to have inscribed his teachings on a bamboo parchment, and these precepts form the basis of Taoist belief. Over the centuries, however, scholars have interpreted and reinterpreted these original sayings, and have built up whole schools of thought and custom on a single phrase, often straying far from early Taoist simplicity. The use of the words "long life" in Lao-tzu's writings led to a quest for elixirs of longevity, and the mention of sexual organs to the development of sexual mysticism. The phrase "breath retention" encouraged the elaboration of techniques of respiratory control akin to yoga and, strangest of all, the words "harmonious infant" led to the idea that one could produce within one's body, and by oneself, an embryonic seed that would be immortal.

Taoism, as we have seen, embraced the idea that there are two basic principles that underlie the Universe: the active force of yang and the equally important passive force of yin. All things were said to be composed of varying proportions of yang and yin. It was believed that men had a greater proportion of yang and women of yin, and that sexual intercourse was a way of achieving harmony between the two principles.

Many magic and occult ideas were gradually absorbed by certain branches of Taoism, and alchemy found a home among these strange and varied beliefs. Unlike their Western counterparts however, Taoist alchemists were less concerned with transmuting base metals to gold. Their prime quest was the secret of immortality. At first they tried mixing various substances in the hope of finding a formula for a magic elixir, but by the 6th century A.D. most alchemists had abandoned the search for an actual elixir. Instead they had begun to concentrate on perfecting certain techniques of sexual control and various breathing exercises. They believed that if an individual was able to attain a true harmony of yang and yin within himself, he would be able to achieve immortality. In order to do this, sexual energies should not be dissipated but should be carefully conserved and converged into higher forms of energy. They thought that man had the power to produce within himself a "harmonious infant," that is, a being on another plane who was somehow attuned to the mysterious workings of the Universe. Taoist alchemists who could produce this divine embryo considered that they had achieved immortality.

The Taoist alchemist visualized the body as having three important psychic centers, which he termed "crucibles." These crucibles were used to store the three main forms of energy. In the lowest crucible at the base of the spine, sexual energy known as *ching* was stored. The second crucible was in the

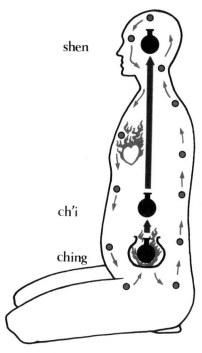

Above: the Taoist subtle body, as seen in the inner alchemy, showing the circulation system. Alchemists start with breathing exercises designed to exert pressure on *ching*, or sexual energy. They then try to activate the second, higher energy *ch'i*. Finally they hope to reach the highest energy, *shen*, in the head. Left: Shou-lao, Tao god of longevity. Taoist alchemists believed that their work could bring immortality. Below: adepts, shown as children, symbolize immortality.

solar plexus behind the stomach. It housed a higher form of energy known as *ch'i*. The top crucible in the head contained the highest form of all, spiritual energy or *shen*.

This inner alchemy was achieved entirely by meditation and breathing. The first stage was known as "lighting the inner fire." The alchemist began deep breathing, which exerted pressure on the lowest crucible containing *ching*, the sexual energy. Heat was generated by breathing and the *ching* rose through the spinal column to the top of the head. It then descended down to the spine again. After this process had been repeated many times, the alchemist might consider the force pure enough to be transformed into a higher form of energy. It would then be driven up into the second crucible where it would mingle with the higher energy *ch'i*. These two combined forces then traveled up to the head and back again, until they in their turn reached a sufficient state of purity to mingle with *shen*, the spiritual force in the top crucible.

These three combined forces rose and fell in the body, gradually becoming purer and purer, until they finally reached a state of oneness with the energies of the Universe. It was then that the divine embryo was conceived. A special ambrosia flowed like saliva into the mouth, and was impregnated by a gold and a silver light. Gradually, nurtured by special concentration and breathing techniques on the part of the alchemist, the embryo grew until it reached maturity. It then ascended into the crown of the head, and the alchemist, turning his attention totally inward, perceived the psychic light that emanated from it. He then believed that he had achieved immortality. The embryo was sent down to the abdomen. The alchemist had completed his task.

This brief description of Taoist inner alchemy bears a striking resemblance to the alchemy developed by the followers of Tantra. Tantra is the name given to a strange set of beliefs practiced for centuries in India and other neighboring countries. Its disciples claim that it is the oldest religion in India, and that all systems of yoga derive from it. Its critics dispute whether it is a religion at all because its ideas are so entwined with strange sexual activity, magic, and the occult.

Tantra is based on the premise that the Universe is composed of a male and a female force. The female force is represented by the goddess Shakti who has an all-important and active role. The passive male force is personified by the god Shiva. He is helpless without Shakti, and man in turn is considered helpless without woman. Women are the key to salvation and it is through women, by ritual sexual intercourse, that the goddess Shakti can be approached. Ritual sexual intercourse may be physical, or may be merely symbolic. Those who choose the physical way are known as followers of the left hand way because the female sexual partner is seated on the left of the male at the start of the ritual. Those who choose the symbolic method are known as followers of the right hand way because the woman sits on the right of the man.

The Tantrist obtains energy through sexual intercourse, in which the woman is regarded as the possessor of important power. Because it is the intercourse itself that is important, and

Above: a 19th-century German drawing after an Indian original, showing the union of the irreconcilables, fire and water. This idea of the union of the opposites was a powerful one in both Western and Eastern alchemy, although in the East it was expressed far more directly in overt sexual terms.

Right: a 16th-century Tibetan statue showing the condition of enlightenment, in which the male and female principles unite in perfect combination. The gods here are Krishna and his consort Radna.

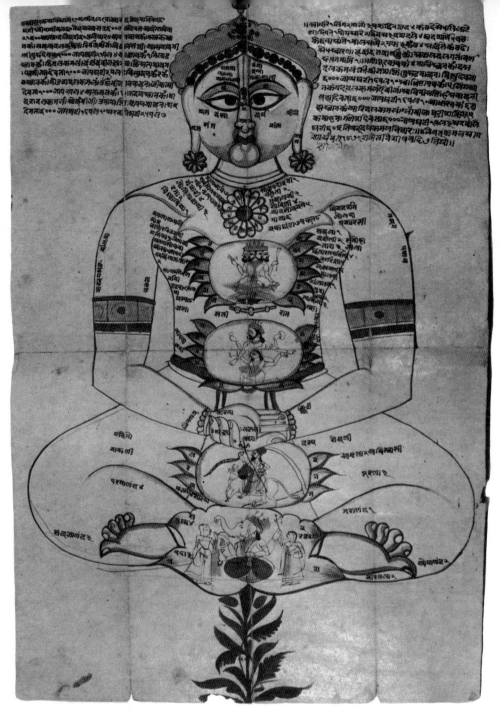

Above: the subtle body, shown as a plant growing from the ground of the beyond, in an Indian 18th-century drawing. The chakras, through which the awakened kundalini would rise, are shown here within the body, with symbolic drawings. Tantric alchemy was emphatic about the great power of the forces aroused through their exercises, and would-be alchemists spent years learning to direct the energies properly toward union with the Infinite.

because its ritual character should be entirely free of any emotional or social connotations, it may be performed with a woman of the lowest caste, and preferably in the most degrading and defiling of conditions. The most powerful rite of all is performed with a woman while she is menstruating, and takes place among the smoldering bodies in a crematory.

Tantra opposes all social conventions and ordinary morality. Many of its sexual rites include group sex, adultery, and incest, which are intended to jolt its followers into a new level of awareness beyond the limitations of family or society. Rather than control or conquer physical desire, the Tantrist believes in releasing sexual energy and then reabsorbing it back into the system in order to gain greater power. The emphasis on various

sexual practices and the link with magic and the occult have brought Tantra into disrepute with more orthodox religions. But it is far from merely being a disguised method of obtaining sexual pleasure. To perform the sexual rites successfully requires years of training in difficult physical techniques. Apart from complex breathing exercises, the Tantrist will aim to control certain seemingly involuntary functions such as the pulse rate and the body temperature. Above all, Tantrists concentrate on alchemy.

Tantric, like Taoist, alchemy is mainly internal. It aims to effect a transmutation in the body by producing certain bodily fluids that will enable the Tantrist to be at one with the Universe, and to acquire supernatural powers. According to the Tantrist, the body has seven main centers of supernormal psychic energy. They have no physical existence, but can be identified by the Tantrist as being situated along a line between the bottom of the spine and the crown of the head. These centers are known as *chakras* or wheels. The lowest chakra is inhabited by the *kundalini*, which in the normal person lies curled up, asleep, like a small serpent, its head blocking the path of ascent to the next *chakra*. If awakened by an inexperienced person, the kundalini will cause havoc and destruction. All kinds of physical energies will be stirred up, and the novice will be unable to control them. The Tantrist takes years of training and discipline before being able to control the aroused kundalini. Once properly awakened, often by various sexual postures, the kundalini is ready to begin its gradual ascent through the chakras, and the process of inner alchemy begins. To aid the ascent the Tantrist will often visualize an ideal woman, since woman holds the key to vital energy. When the kundalini reaches the uppermost chakra in the crown of the head, the alchemist has achieved the goal. Shakti and Shiva, the two principles of the Universe, are fused in a transcendental sexual union, and supreme ecstasy is attained. Transmutation has taken place in the desired spiritual way. The self is at one with the Infinite.

While Eastern alchemists were concerned with internal or sexual alchemy, their Western counterparts, as we already know, were pursuing different aims. They were searching for the Philosopher's Stone, which they believed could turn base metals to gold, and for spiritual perfection. Neither of these aims had any clear sexual element. But in the 18th and 19th centuries ideas from the East began to trickle through, and Western writers began to look at sex in a new light. They began to consider that perhaps a sexual motivation lay behind many aspects of human behavior, previously accepted at face value, and they began to see sexual symbolism in many ordinary objects of use.

These ideas gradually affected alchemy which, in the face of growing materialism and the achievements of scientific chemistry, was fast becoming a mystical rite. Just as astronomy had grown out of astrology and left the older system of thought to the occultists, so had the scientists deserted alchemy and left it to those more attuned to the supernatural.

So it was that Dr. W. R. Woodman and Dr. Wynn Westcott, two English physicians who were interested in alchemy, joined

Below: a Tantric yogi seated in his meditation band, a 17th-century stone statuette from South India. Of course, all the exercises of the Tantrist were not sexual; a great deal of solitary meditation and physical and breathing exercises were a vital part of the philosophy.

Right: a certificate of membership in the Ordo Templis Orientis, usually known simply as OTO. The society, which attempted to incorporate sexual alchemy within the magical tradition, was first established by Kark Kellner, a German who went to India to study Tantric sexual alchemy. He was one of the first to bring its teachings back to western Europe.

forces with Samuel Liddell Macgregor Mathers, a strange figure who became well known in occult circles, to found the Hermetic Order of the Golden Dawn in 1888. The Golden Dawn was a secret society whose members studied the Cabala, divination, ritual magic, and other occult subjects including alchemy.

Westcott had been influenced by the writings of Ethan Allen Hitchcock, an American who, he believed, "furnishes us the key to the understanding of the hermetic masters. The subject is man . . . The work of the alchemists was one of contemplation and not a work of the hands. Their alembic, furnace, cucurbit, retort, philosophical Egg . . . in which the work of fermentation, distillation, extraction of essences and spirits, and the preparation of salts is said to have taken place was Man . . ." This idea was one that proved immensely attractive to late 19th- and early 20th-century occultists. Discoveries by scientists about the nature of matter appeared to have demolished the idea of a Philosopher's Stone, but if the true aim of alchemy

could be seen as a change within a person, then the way was wide open to new spiritual, sexual, or psychological interpretations of alchemy.

Ithell Colquhoun, a member of a group much influenced by the Golden Dawn, unequivocally identified the objects of alchemy with those of sex. She maintained that the alembic was the uterus and the bath of Venus was the vagina. "Moderate fire" referred to the sexual heat of the body, and aqua vitae to female secretions.

A sexual alchemy even more directly related to Eastern mysticism was developed by Karl Kellner. He was a wealthy German who had spent many years in India at the end of the 19th century studying the secrets of Tantric sexual alchemy. On his return to Germany he suggested to various friends who were already interested in the occult that they form a secret society to incorporate Tantric beliefs and practices. In 1902 he and others formed the *Ordo Templis Orientis*, or Order of the Templars of the East. It was devoted to sexual magic. There were nine degrees of sexual ritual to be mastered, the highest being the sexual union of the Tantric alchemist. Members claimed that sexual magic was the key to all the secrets of the Universe and to all the symbolism ever used by secret societies and religions. In the ritual of the Order of the Templars of the East, traditional Western alchemy was given a sexual interpretation. The athanor, the alchemist's most important furnace, symbolized the phallus. The serpent, or blood of the Red Lion, was the semen. The cucurbit stood for the vagina, and the mysterious first matter of the alchemists was composed of vaginal secretions mixed with semen. Franz Hartmann, one of the founder members of the Order, saw the base metals used in alchemy as the animal driving forces in human nature which were capable of being transformed into pure spirituality—or the true gold of the alchemist.

Other interpretations of alchemy have been made by 20th-century psychologists. One of the greatest of these, Carl Jung, devoted many years of his life to a study of alchemy. He noticed that many alchemical symbols occurred in the dreams of his patients, and in mythologies and religions throughout the world. He came to the conclusion that these symbols stemmed from a common source that he termed "the collective unconscious." This level of the mind is made up not of personal experiences, but of archetypes, which are the distilled memories, in some way inherited, of human experience many thousands of years ago. These archetypes are too far out of reach of the conscious mind to be expressed in words. In certain universal situations such as danger, conflict, or desire, however, they will struggle to find expression by means of symbols. These symbols are common to peoples who have had no contact with each other and who, one might think, have had no particular experience that might lead to the choice of such a specific image. Jung's belief was that if we could learn to recognize what the symbols stood for, we might become more in tune with our own unconscious and hence lead a fuller and more integrated life. The alchemical symbols can therefore be interpreted as providing a clue to our truer nature. The image of the hermaphrodite so

Below: an illustration from a book by Franz Hartmann, one of the founding members of the OTO, which shows the traditional Philosopher's Egg with the symbols of the zodiac inside it.

Above: Carl Jung (left), the great psychologist, was particularly attracted by the symbolism of alchemy, finding within its images many of the archetypes he believed were embedded deep within mankind's collective unconscious, beyond conscious memory.

Above: a hermaphrodite, from an alchemical book published in 1572. The symbol, which Jung recognized as an archetype, was used to represent the union of opposites.

commonly used in alchemy, for example, indicates the female side of man's nature, and the male side of woman's, which must be recognized rather than suppressed.

Jung's idea of a "complete self" was one in which all the opposing forces in human nature, conscious and unconscious, had become reconciled so that the person was at one with himself. In alchemy, in the idea of the Philosopher's Stone, he found the same ideal of a reconciliation of opposites that would result in something of far greater power than the mere addition of the two separate forces. Symbolic descriptions of the Philosopher's Stone suggest this union. It has been described as being made of fire and water, as the masculine-feminine, and as a stone and not a stone. It has been symbolized as the marriage of the king and queen, the sun and moon, and the fair white woman and the ruddy man. It has also been seen in terms of incest between brother and sister and between mother and son.

Herbert Silberer, a German psychologist, has taken this interpretation of incest even more literally. In his book *The Hidden Symbolism of Alchemy*, published in 1917, he examines a vision

recorded by the earliest known alchemical writer, Zosimos of Egypt. This dream describes a ritual involving a priest and resulting in much blood and sacrifice. It has generally been taken to symbolize the various alchemical stages in the transmutation of base metals to gold. Silberer, however, sees the dream of Zosimos in terms of sexual symbolism. He comes to the conclusion that the alchemical quest represented no more or less than the lifelong penance of the son for his childhood urge to castrate his father and replace him in his mother's bed.

All these varying interpretations of alchemy may seem confusing, but one thing is clear. Alchemy represents a long and difficult search for a key to understand the mysterious workings of the Universe. The route chosen is often that most suited to the society in which the alchemist is living. The East, with its tradition of yoga and meditation, developed a system of internal sexual alchemy. To the Medieval Western alchemist the idea of a Philosopher's Stone that would transmute base metals to gold was in accordance with many of the beliefs of the time. The 20th-century Westerner interested in alchemy will probably find a psychological or sexual interpretation more relevant.

Above: another example of the hermaphrodite, used here as the symbol for the process in the Work when a substance combined of opposites is placed in the fire.

8

Alchemy Lives On

After the physical and chemical discoveries of the 18th and 19th centuries, it would have seemed natural for alchemy in the 20th century to have advanced ever farther into the realms of symbolism and mysticism, and away from anything to do with physical transmutation. But in 1919 the eminent English physicist Lord Rutherford succeeded in transmuting nitrogen into oxygen in the laboratory, and every aspiring alchemist took new heart. Admittedly, the quantity of oxygen produced was hardly impressive, and the experiment involved the use of high-energy radioactivity. But at least it refuted the continual insistence by scientists that

Although the 17th century saw traditional alchemy move away from the laboratory into the rarefied regions of mystical and magical speculation, the 20th-century alchemists seem to be returning to their laboratories with renewed enthusiasm, using the technical expertise that has been gathered in the inter-vening years by orthodox chemists.

Right: a modern Iranian alchemist at work on the age-old goal of transmuting base metals to gold.

"When the crucible was broken, a nugget of gold was found inside..."

transmutation was an impossibility. One of the first to take inspiration and renewed hope from this experiment was Franz Tausend, a 36-year-old chemical assistant in Munich. He had developed his own theories about the structure of chemical elements. These were a strange mixture of the beliefs of the Greek philosopher Pythagoras about the structure of the Universe, and the findings of the Russian chemist Mendeleev in 1863. Mendeleev devised a way of classifying chemical elements by arranging them in order of their atomic weights, and discovered that chemically similar elements recurred at approximately equal intervals or periods. This became known as the *Periodic System.* Tausend wrote a pamphlet, *180 Elements, the Atomic Weight, and their incorporation in the System of Harmonic Periods,* on his theories. His belief was that every atom of an element had a characteristic frequency of vibration, which was related to the atomic weight of the nucleus and the various orbital rings of electrons around it. Later research was to show that this part of Tausend's theory was true. He went on, however, to suggest that matter could be as it were "orchestrated." By this he meant adding a carefully selected substance to one element to change its vibration frequency into that of another.

At about this time in 1924 Adolf Hitler was sent to jail for organizing an armed rising in Munich. His fellow conspirator, General Erich von Ludendorff, was acquitted. In the following year Ludendorff ran for election as president of the German republic, but he was heavily defeated in the polls by General Hindenburg. He then turned his attention to fund-raising for the Nazis. He heard the rumors that a certain Tausend in Munich had succeeded in making gold, and got together a party of associates to visit Tausend. The group consisted of Kummer, a chemical engineer, Alfred Mannesmann, a business magnate, Osthoff, a banker, Stremmel, a merchant, and a fifth man known as Franz von Rebay. Stremmel had bought the necessary substances, largely iron oxide and quartz, on Tausend's instructions. He had them melted down by Kummer and von Rebay, and took the crucible to his hotel bedroom in Munich for the night so that no one could tamper with it. In the morning, Tausend heated the crucible again in the electric furnace, added a small quantity of a white powder to the molten mass, and allowed it to cool. When the crucible was broken, a nugget of gold weighing seven grams was found inside.

Ludendorff then formed a company called Company 164 with himself at its head. He was to receive 75 percent of the profits, and Tausend five percent. Investments poured in, of which Ludendorff succeeded in diverting some 400,000 marks "to patriotic ends"—the financing of the Nazi party. This affected the company adversely. In December 1926 he resigned as the company head and restored all rights to Tausend, but left him to shoulder all the debts. Tausend continued to raise money, however, and on June 16, 1928 is said to have made 723 grams of gold in a single large-scale operation. No doubt it was this success that encouraged him to issue a series of share certificates, each to the value of 10 kilograms of gold.

But time was running out for Tausend. A year later, when no more gold had been produced, he was arrested for fraud. After

Above: Franz Tausend, the modern German alchemist who claimed in the 1920s that he had been totally successful in changing iron oxide and quartz to gold. Although there were many who claimed that he was entirely fraudulent, the evidence is ambiguous, and there were certainly some who were convinced that he had done what he said.

Above: the extensive laboratory and factory in which Tausend
worked on his gold-making project, during the period in which
General Erich von Ludendorff was involved with the enterprise.
Right: General von Ludendorff, the World War I military
leader. His interest in Tausend was strictly to raise money
for the Nazi cause to which he had become completely converted.

a long wait in prison and a sensational trial, he was found guilty
on February 5, 1931, and sentenced to nearly four years' imprisonment. While awaiting trial, he had allegedly made gold
under supervision at the Munich Mint—but experts disagreed
so violently on what had happened that the evidence was of no
value in court.

In the same year, a Polish engineer named Dunikovski announced in Paris that he had discovered a new kind of radiation
that he named "Z rays." He said these rays would transmute
sand or quartz into gold. The mineral was ground up, spread
on copper plates, and melted by application of 110,000 volts.
Then it was irradiated by Dunikovski's Z rays.

The engineer succeeded in raising an investment of some two
million francs. When after a few months he had not produced
any gold, he, like Tausend, was brought to trial for fraud. In
due course he was found guilty and sent to jail for four years.
After two years his lawyer succeeded in obtaining his release,
and in 1934 Dunikovski took his family to San Remo, a seaside
town in Italy, where he renewed his experiments.

Soon rumors began to reach Paris that the engineer was supporting his wife and children by the occasional sale of lumps of
gold. His lawyer, accompanied by the well-known French
chemist Albert Bonn, traveled to San Remo to see for himself.

Above: Dunikovski, the Polish engineer. While he was living in Italy in the 1930s rumors began that he was successfully extracting gold from sand, using what he called "embryonic atoms," which he believed exist in all minerals.

They discovered that the sand that Dunikovski was using in his experiments contained a small proportion of gold, but whereas normal methods of extraction yielded only some 10 grams of gold per ton, Dunikovski's method produced nearly 100 times as much. This sounds impressive, but it must be remembered that, since each experiment involved only a few hundred grams of sand, the quantity of gold being extracted was extremely small.

Nevertheless, the two Frenchmen were sufficiently impressed to ask the French government to reopen the Dunikovski case. On March 26, 1935, Dunikovski himself addressed an open letter to the prime minister, offering the French government a first option on his invention. The French newspapers, however, opposed the idea vociferously.

In October 1936 Dunikovski gave a demonstration to an audience of invited scientists. He was naturally secretive about the details of his apparatus, but the theoretical explanation he gave is interesting in that it went right back to the primitive beginnings of alchemy. He believed that all minerals contained atoms in the course of transformation, a process that takes thousands of years in nature. He called these atoms "embryonic atoms," and claimed that his process accelerated the growth of the embryonic gold in quartz.

The demonstration attracted a great deal of attention. Mussolini instructed an Italian professor to look into the process. Paris financiers retained the chemist Coupie. An Anglo-French syndicate was formed. Sand was to be brought from Africa and treated in a big new laboratory in England.

Then came World War II. There were stories that a factory for transmuting base metals into gold had been established in Saint Blaise on the French–Swiss border. Rumor further insisted that the Germans had found some way to bolster their sinking economy by the manufacture of gold. But no proof has ever been found. Meanwhile in England, in a crammed laboratory in the center of London, a modern alchemist claimed to have made the Philosopher's Stone.

His name was Archibald Cockren. He had qualified as an osteopath in London in 1904. During World War I he had been in charge of the department of electrical massage and remedial treatment, first at the Russian Hospital in London, and then at the Prisoners of War Hospital. Later he had been attached to the Australian Army, and served on the staff of the Australian prime minister at the peace conference. He was clearly a respected and responsible practitioner.

He spent the next 20 years in private practice. During this period it became fairly common to inject gold salts as a cure for rheumatism and arthritis, and Cockren became very interested in such gold therapy. He also experimented with homeopathic methods of healing by making use of microscopic doses of gold. Looking for new ways to make solutions of compounds of gold, he decided to try to prepare the "oil of gold" of which so many alchemists had written.

Cockren had read *The Triumphal Chariot of Antimony* by Basil Valentine, a strange figure whose true identity lies hidden in the alchemical legends of the 15th and 16th centuries. Valentine is credited with the discovery of the element anti-

mony. He was supposed to have given it the name *antimoine*, which in French would mean "against a monk," because he had used it successfully to poison several monks. Whatever the truth of the legend, Cockren decided to begin his experiments with antimony. He managed to produce a "fragrant golden liquid." Then he went on to work with iron and copper. "The oil of these metals was obtained, a few drops of which used singly, or in conjunction, proved very efficacious in cases of anemia and debility." He related how, on one occasion, he took a few drops of the oil himself after a particularly laborious day, and found himself reinvigorated. The prospect of a "bout of fairly strenuous mental effort held no terrors at all."

After continuing his experiments with silver and mercury, Cockren finally turned his attention to gold; but he found that his watery mixture would not retain gold in solution. He realized that what he lacked was the "alkahest of the philosophers," the universal solvent that alchemists believed would dissolve all matter. Only with this, thought Cockren, could he achieve the real oil of gold. He plunged into a study of alchemical writings, anxious to find a clue to the identity of this strange solvent. The experiments he had already made helped considerably. One day, while sitting quietly in a state of deep concentration, the solution to the problem was revealed to him in a flash, and he suddenly understood many of the puzzling statements of the alchemists.

"Here, then, I entered upon a new course of experiment with a metal for experimental purposes with which I had no previous experience. The metal, after being reduced to its salts and undergoing special preparation and distillation, delivered up the Mercury of the Philosophers."

The first intimation Cockren had that he had been successful was a violent hissing. Jets of vapor poured from the retort and into the receiver "like sharp bursts from a machine gun." Then there was a violent explosion and "a very potent and subtle odor filled the laboratory and its surroundings." A friend of Cockren's described this odor as resembling "the dry earth on a June morning, with the hint of growing flowers in the air, the breath of wind over heather and hill, and the sweet smell of rain on the parched earth."

Cockren's next problem was to find a way of storing this "subtle gas" without endangering anything. He achieved this by an arrangement of coils of glass piping in water joined up with the receiver, and a carefully regulated system of heating. The result was that the gas gradually condensed into a clear golden "water" that was extremely inflammable and volatile. The water then had to be separated by distillation, "the outcome being the white mercurial water." This mercurial water, added Cockren, was absolutely essential to the production of the oil of gold. It was added to the salts of gold after the salts had been washed several times with distilled water to remove the acidity of the Aqua Regia, a mixture of nitric and hydrochloric acid that had been used to dissolve the gold. He found that when the mercurial water was added to the salts of gold, there was a slight hissing sound and an increase in temperature, after which the gold became a deep red liquid. When this was distilled the

The Fragrant Explosion

Archibald Cockren believed fully that behind alchemy's transmutation of metals lay the transmutation of the baser elements in the human. But he also believed that the work in the laboratory could be accomplished. Using the texts of the alchemists and putting aside his own knowledge of more orthodox chemistry, Cockren set about the Great Work in his 20th-century London laboratory.

Following the 12 Keys of Basil Valentine, he began experimenting with antimony, but realized that he had still not grasped what was meant by the First Matter. The answer came to him suddenly, full-blown— although he does not say what it was. He started work again with a metal he had not used before.

Cockren went through the old series of stages—the reduction to its salts, heating, distillation—and then suddenly he knew he had achieved success. There was a violent hissing, and jets of vapor poured out of the retort and into the receiver with a series of loud noises like machine gun shots. The whole apparatus exploded, and a strange fragrance filled the laboratory: the fresh smell of the earth on a June morning, with dew, flowers, and gentle wind. He had made the Mercury of the Philosophers.

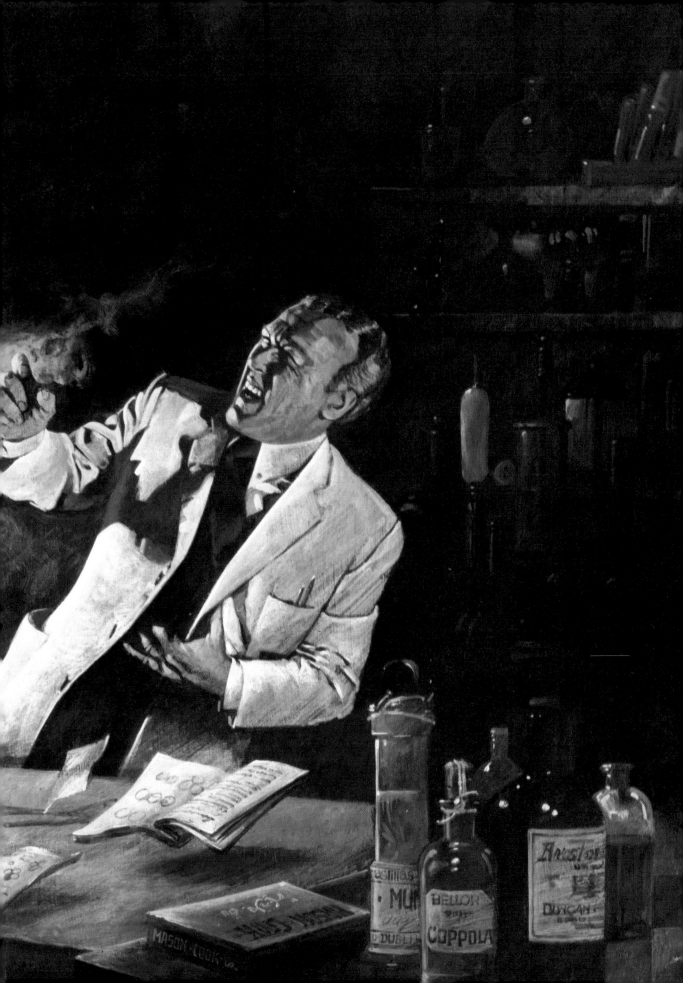

Above: Eugene Canseliet, the well-known French alchemist and writer on alchemy. Like many of the contemporary alchemists, he has returned to work in the laboratory.

oil of gold, a deep amber liquid of an oily consistency, was produced. "From the golden water I have described can be obtained this white water, and a deep red tincture which deepens in color the longer it is kept; these two are the mercury and the sulfur described by the alchemists."

To make the Philosopher's Stone, Cockren took the black dregs of the metal left after the extraction of the golden water, heated it to red hot, and then treated it until it became a white salt. He then took a certain quantity of this "salt" and of the "mercury" and "sulfur" that he had already produced, and put them in a hermetically sealed flask over a moderate heat. The mixture looked at first like leaden mud, which slowly rose like dough until it produced a crystalline formation "rather like a coral plant in growth." Edward Garstin, a writer and friend of Cockren's, visited him at this time and saw "a glass vessel of oval shape containing layer upon layer of basic matter in the traditional colors of black, white, gray, and yellow. At the top these had blossomed into a flower-like form, a pattern arranged like petals around a center, all of a glowing orange-scarlet."

The heat was gradually raised until this formation melted into an amber-colored liquid, which then thickened and sank into a black earth on the bottom of the glass. "When more mercury was added, the black powder dissolved and from this conjunction it seems that a new substance is born . . . As the black color abates, color after color comes and goes until the mixture becomes white and shining; the White Elixir. The heat is gradually

raised yet more, and from white the color changes to citrine and finally to red—the Elixir Vitae, the Philosopher's Stone, the medicine of men and metals."

Soon after this, Cockren was killed in the blitz of London, and his secret perished with him. He left many who believed in the curative powers of his oil of gold. Mrs. Maiya Tranchell Hayes, who headed a surviving temple of the Golden Dawn, swore by it, as did Mrs. Meyer Sassoon, widow of a well-known financier. As late as 1965 there were elderly people in London who still took small doses of Cockren's elixir.

Since the war, most alchemical speculation seems to have taken place in France. Eugene Canseliet, who has written many books on alchemy, has been seen on television at work in his laboratory. Others, like the author Roger Caro and the painter Louis Cattiaux, have also established laboratories. But the most famous French alchemist is probably Armand Barbault, author of *Gold of a Thousand Mornings*. He carries out his work only at times that he has determined by detailed astrological calculation.

Perhaps Barbault gained his initial inspiration from a well-known theory that the name of the Rosicrucians is derived not from *rosa*, the Latin word for rose, but from *ros*, the Latin word for dew. An essential part of his process, for example, is the gathering of dew in canvas sheets every morning from March 21 to June 24. The idea of gathering dew was first put forward at the end of the 17th century in a mysterious book of engravings without captions entitled *Mutus Liber*, the *Wordless Book*. The author of another book of about the same date, the *Polygraphice*, writes: "Gather Dew in the Month of May, with a clean white Linnen Cloth spread upon the Grass." When this filtered dew has been left for 14 days in horse dung, and then distilled to a quarter of its bulk four times running, it yields a potent Spirit of Dew. "And if you are indeed an Artist, you may by this turn all Metals into their first matter."

Barbault describes his first matter as a germ, growing a few centimeters below the surface in black earth in a woodland clearing. This substance, whatever it is, is placed in a closed flask, kept at a steady temperature of 40°C (104°F). Dew, in which the tips of young plants have been fermented for 40 days, is added through a faucet. As far as it is possible to make out from Barbault's erratic account, the final ingredient is a "mother plant." There are detailed instructions on how to draw this plant whole from the ground by tying one end of a string to it, and the other end of the string to a nearby bush that has been bent over. The bush is then released, and as it springs back to place, it pulls the plant out.

The flask is kept at the temperature of 40°C (104°F) for 40 days, extra dew being added as necessary. Later, the temperature is raised until a dry ash is obtained. This is then put into long test tubes, together with about 2.5 grams of powdered gold and some dew, and the tubes are sealed with a rubber stopper. Barbault has a thermostatically controlled oven maintained at a temperature between 150° and 200°C (302° and 392°F)—that is, substantially above the boiling point of water—and 12 test tubes are inserted partway into this oven so that the contents

Above: Armand Barbault at work. He began as an engineer, but through his interest in astrology was drawn—encouraged by his wife—into an exploration of the practical possiblities of alchemy.

Right: wringing the morning dew out of the canvas spread to collect it, from *The Wordless Book*. Barbault followed this example in his own alchemical work, collecting dew every day before sunrise for three months, as instructed. Below: Barbault collecting dew. *The Wordless Book* showed the collection from canvas spread on the grass, but Barbault found much more dew could be gathered by dragging the sheet along the ground, over the tops of plants.

Right: wringing out the heavily dew-laden canvasses. According to Barbault, the quality of the dew depends on the kind of plant from which it has been collected.

boil. The steam condenses in the upper part of the tubes, which are outside the oven, and liquid returns to solid matter below. After four hours of boiling, and four hours of standing, repeated seven times, the liquor in the tubes is a clear golden color—but, says Barbault, spectrum analysis does not reveal the presence of any gold in solution.

Armand Barbault regards this liquor as the alchemists' elixir, and calls it vegetable gold. It seems, in fact, to be a typical homeopathic remedy effective in microscopic doses. Dr. Ruth Jensen-Hillringhaus of Freiburg, Germany claimed to have used it to cure a woman paralyzed by multiple sclerosis. Another doctor tried several drops of the elixir each morning and reported a marked reduction in tiredness, increase in initiative, and improved urination. Others reported miracle cures of uremia and syphilis. Barbault, who found it too expensive to

Right: Armand Barbault in his modern laboratory. As a 20th-century alchemist, he uses the conveniences developed since the times of the medieval workers. All the heating is controlled by thermostats, and many of the operations are fully automatic. Below: Barbault's starting point is a mixture of earth and plants. It is moistened with the dew, baked in the alembic, remoistened, and the process is repeated until this black substance is produced.

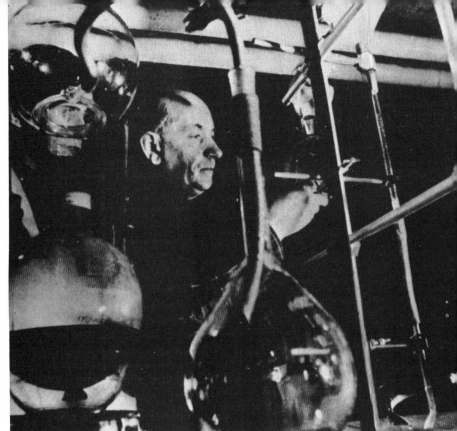

Right: the liquor of gold. After it has been produced, it is carefully checked over a week to be sure it is free of impurities. Only then can it be used as the alchemists' elixir. A few drops are claimed to work wonders in curing a variety of diseases.

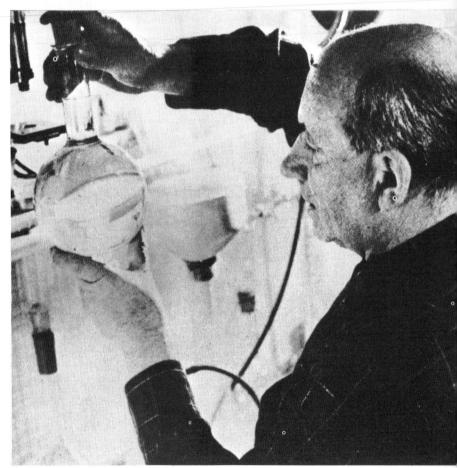

continue adding gold to his liquors, was last reported to be employing the "Blood of the Green Lion"—extracted vegetable sap.

The story of alchemy is like a detective novel. But, although in this last chapter it is possible to unravel some of the tangled threads and make some deductions, there can be no dramatic last-minute revelation. We can only guess at the possible nature of first matter and the Philosopher's Stone.

We do not know whether seemingly objective scientific witnesses ever saw a real transmutation in an alchemist's laboratory, but we do know that transmutation is possible. It goes on naturally all the time as radioactive elements decay and give off radiation—and the end-product of this "putrefaction" is lead. Transmutation is also possible in a modern laboratory. Apart from the changes from one known element to another, as in Rutherford's experiment, there are more than a dozen new elements known to science which do not occur naturally at all, but which have been made in the course of experiments in nuclear energy. The only limitation to laboratory transmutation at the moment is that subatomic particles that travel at high speeds and with immense energies are needed.

Alchemical tests are full of tantalizing information about the nature of first matter. This desirable substance is, apparently, to be found everywhere, is walked on by everybody, prized by nobody. Quartz and sand, the essential ingredients of both Tausend's and Dunikovski's process, answer well to this description. These minerals are almost pure silicon dioxide, and it is possible that when Cockren spoke of using "a metal . . . with which I had had no previous experience," he was referring to silicon. This element is not in fact a metal. However it is known as a metalloid because in its physical nature and chemical properties it belongs to a group of elements including germanium, tin, and lead, and of which the first member is carbon. Silicon is of particular interest in that it can take the place of carbon in a great number of chemical compounds, producing silicones. It has even been suggested that life, which on Earth is sustained by compounds of carbon, may be sustained by silicones on some other planet in another galaxy.

This is as far as the clues in our detective story lead us. It is disappointing not to be able to conclude by unmasking an alchemical "butler," but our present-day knowledge of the nature of matter is still too sketchy. It may be naive to suppose that any alchemist ever succeeded in preparing gold by transmutation, although the possibility exists; but there seems every reason to believe that, by some means that we still call magic, men were able to perceive a vision of what we are only just beginning to discover by experiment. They told their vision in a succession of charming allegorical stories. The birth of metals and their progression through seven stages to the perfection of gold paralleled the seven ages of man, or the passing of the soul through the seven planetary spheres to heaven. The quest for the Philosopher's Stone and the Elixir of Life obsessed and impoverished many alchemists—but it is possible that they knew something that our modern scientists are only just beginning to discover.

Right: Saturn, symbolizing lead, is cooked in a bath until the white dove, or spirit, ascends. By the bath the earnest alchemist puffs away at the bellows. Behind the elegant imagery, and the carefully obscure texts, still lies the tantalizing mystery of alchemy. After all these centuries it still fascinates, still obsesses people by the ancient promise of untold riches and the hope of spiritual fulfillment.

Picture Credits